AN OUTLINE OF
SHETLAND ARCHAEOLOGY

AN OUTLINE OF
SHETLAND ARCHAEOLOGY

John Stewart

a reprint of the series of articles first published in
August and September, 1956, in *The Shetland Times*

Shetland Amenity Trust
2008

An Outline of Shetland Archaeology, 2008.

Copyright © 2008 Shetland Amenity Trust and representatives of the late John Stewart.

ISBN 978 0 9557642 2 6

First published by Shetland Amenity Trust, 2008.

All rights reserved.
No part of this publication may be reproduced, stored in a retrieval system, or transmitted, in any form, or by any means, electronic, mechanical, photocopying, recording or otherwise, without the prior written permission of the publishers.

A CIP catalogue record for this book is available from the British Library.

Printed by
Shetland Litho,
Gremista, Lerwick,
Shetland ZE1 0PX.

CONTENTS

Foreword	....	vii
Chapter 1	Before Christ	1
Chapter 2	The Brochs and After	13
Chapter 3	The Norse Invasion	27
Chapter 4	The Evidence of Place Names	43
Chapter 5	Norse and Christian Remains	49
Appendix I	....	57
Appendix II	....	61
Appendix III	Museums	63
Appendix IV	....	65
Appendix V	....	69

Foreword

"THE main purpose of archaeology" concluded John Stewart at the end of "An Outline of Shetland Archaeology" "is ... to map and describe accurately all finds from prehistory, so that a body of knowledge may be built up of how people lived in the many centuries which are gone. In the evidence still existing of these centuries Shetland is one of the fortunate lands."

Quite independently, I wrote recently that "the main purpose of archaeology is to establish how we today have got to where we are now and to understand and appreciate the skills and knowledge of our ancestors" – which is remarkably similar, albeit fifty years later. The results of archaeology, provided that these are made as accessible to non-specialists as possible, help to create a rooted-ness and pride of place. It is undisputed that the past is a major part of what makes Shetland what it is today. It is after all uniquely our past. In the same way as it is important to know about our distant roots, so it is also important to understand why we think what we think. How did our thoughts and views about these roots, which we sometimes regard as the "truth" and frequently debate (for we only see through a glass darkly), develop?

Remembering where archaeological thought in Shetland began is therefore a compelling reason to republish John Stewart's "Outline of Shetland Archaeology" fifty years after it was first published. Stewart made the first attempt to write a chronological narrative that specifically told the story of *Shetland's* past from earliest times. It began as a series of articles which were published in "The Shetland Times" in 1956.

There have been notable antiquarians who worked in, and wrote about, specific investigations which they had made into Shetland sites, particularly Gilbert Goudie, and Hamilton's ground breaking "Jarlshof" report was published in the same year (1956). The Royal Commission on Ancient and Historical Monuments' Shetland volume, published in 1946, also preceded Stewart's volume. However, Shetland was somewhat short changed in this gazetteer of sites, due both to the onset of war and to the considerable resources which would have been required to comprehensively visit all the mapped Shetland sites which were at a distance from the road or on islands difficult of access. Calder, who had been tasked with wrapping up, rather than finishing off, the Shetland volume in the 1930s, had become aware of the large numbers and remarkable preservation of unrecorded prehistoric house sites in Shetland. He therefore returned in the 1950s in order to rectify the situation.

At that time, Stewart, a teacher in Aberdeen home for the summer, was inspired to begin excavation at the Beenie, or Bunyie, Hoose on Pettigarth's field in his home island of Whalsay. Stewart spent many years excavating the site prior to 1954 and 1955 when Calder joined him to complete the excavation of the "Hoose". Stewart subsequently excavated the nearby burial sites. The records from that excavation are truly remarkable. Calder published their discoveries in the Proceedings of the Society of Antiquaries 1960-61. One of the outstanding features of that publication is the standard of the drawn plans which included "concentric rings" which were faithfully reproduced. In the light of what we know now, these "rings" almost certainly represent different phases of building and rebuilding, changing as fashion, and perhaps also the need for repair, dictated. These drawings alone would stand as a remarkable tribute to this pair, for what can be more important than that the archaeologist should record all the evidence. Whether or not the archaeologist fully understands what it means, or interprets it in a way which is later shown to be incorrect, is of far less consequence than the fact that the detail is recorded for all time. Stewart and Calder were setting new standards of recording. Surely this is the highest accolade that can bestowed on any archaeologist: that their records are a true and faithful portrayal of the evidence; records which will stand the test of time regardless of ever changing perceptions and understanding that future archaeologists may bring to them.

However John Stewart had begun his excavations before he met Calder. The earliest dated record of his work, held in the Shetland Archives, is a "Report on a Cairn from the West side Houll Loch, Whalsay" written in August 1935. This was followed by a number of other reports and records of his discoveries. Stewart was also one of a group of Shetland scholars who regularly debated their views in the columns of the

"Shetland News". Stewart's first academic publication was a joint venture with Peter Moar in 1944, entitled "Newly discovered sculptured stones from Papil, Shetland" which was published in the "Proceedings of the Society of Antiquaries of Scotland". Stewart also contributed both historical articles and short stories frequently to the "New Shetlander". The first Viking Congress was held in Lerwick in July 1950 and Stewart gave a paper on "Udal Law and Government in Shetland". It is a comment on the industry of the man that his Pettigarth's Field excavations must have been more or less concurrent with the start of his massive project to record the place names of Shetland, which began in 1950.

How we interpret evidence, and what we now believe to be true about Shetland Archaeology, have evolved rapidly during the last two decades and are still constantly changing. Indeed the first attempt to bring Stewart's "Outline" up to date was made by Noel Fojut whose booklet "Prehistoric and Viking Shetland" was first published in 1981. This is now in its fifth edition (2006), each one having been substantially rewritten and expanded in order to keep it current. My own volume, "Ancient Shetland" published in 1997, was designed to give a rather more detailed picture than any of its predecessors but this would now also need a major re-write before being reprinted, such is the rate of new knowledge which is being accrued through major projects such as Old Scatness Broch and Viking Unst as well as the many smaller excavations which have taken place throughout the islands during the past 20 years.

In considering what to include in this foreword I have rejected the temptation to go through the booklet theory by theory and comment on whether archaeologists today would agree, disagree or debate and why. That would require an entire book in itself and would also be bound by the limits of today's knowledge in the same way as Stewart was. Suffice to say that Stewart's book contains examples of all three. However, I have to raise a cheer that Stewart championed the theory that brochs originated in the north: a theory which became very unfashionable until recent excavations at Old Scatness (and a 1970s excavation at the Bu in Orkney which was generally disregarded) lent considerable weight to this theory. Stewart lamented that there was a complete lack of dates available to him. At the time, radiocarbon dating was at its inception. These days we have such an abundance of dating techniques at our disposal that, in some respects, we are now working in a very different arena.

"An Outline" ends with the appeal for a museum for Shetland; something which we know with the benefit of hindsight, was to come to fruition only a few years later. In the absence of one, Stewart advocated sending artefacts to the National Museum at Queen Street (with its wonderful "stone room") which itself no longer exists. Today we have the second Shetland Museum, combined with the Archives at Hays Dock, the repository for the artefacts from more recent excavations.

Stewart was the perhaps the first person to set down some of the ideas about archaeology which are still rehearsed today in contribution to debate about the past. He also highlighted Calder's work on prehistoric houses which would otherwise have been confined to professional circles. These provide good reasons to republish "An Outline" and to make it available for readers today. Sometimes, however, Stewart got it resoundingly wrong! Hoping to deter treasure hunters from digging into remains he wrote "There is no chance whatever of finding anything of value". Two years later the St Ninian's Isle Treasure was discovered! Shetland's Archaeology has continued to flourish and reveal treasures: not usually of intrinsic value but certainly of national and international importance. Stewart's final claim that "In the evidence still existing of these centuries Shetland is one of the fortunate lands" is even more true than it ever was. And fortunate are we who follow on from the legacy which Stewart and his compatriots have left to us.

Val Turner
Shetland Archaeologist
February 2008

Chapter 1

Before Christ

UNTIL the First World War no one set foot on Shetland who had not come by water, and even the seaplanes which first made the journey by air in 1917 had to take off and alight on the sea. And as the sea can be crossed in any direction without let or hindrance, it is worth while finding out who our neighbours are, for Shetland's role in history has been determined by three factors, her proximity to certain countries, her use of them and their possession of the necessary motive and sufficient skill in seamanship to reach her shores and take advantage of her resources.

From Sumburgh Head to North Ronaldsay in Orkney is 47 miles, with Fair Isle in the middle, a few miles nearer to Shetland. This is the only route where it is possible to observe land continuously, though not indeed at sea level. So, while Iceland was discovered by accident and New Zealand by castaways, it may be reasonable to suppose that the majority of Shetland immigrants used this route of set purpose, observing land ahead and following it to its end. Where there was no land ahead there was no voyaging, and Faroe and Iceland had to remain empty until the ninth century AD. The voyage of Pytheas of 320 BC to Thule, which was six days' sail from Britain, where it was neither land, sea or air, but a mixture of all three, and where the inhabitants brewed drink from grain and honey, seems to indicate some early knowledge of Norway, though there is no evidence in archaeology that there was any contact of peoples until the migration period which led to the colonising of Faroe and Iceland.

The truth is that one can coast to Shetland from Scotland without being at any time more than twelve miles from land, for North Ronaldsay is merely 24 miles from Fair Isle and Sumburgh Head is but 20. The weather in summer for long periods offers no impediment to navigation, even with primitive craft; although sudden storms, the dreaded tides of the Pentland and Sumburgh Roost and many unknown but no less dangerous island sounds, and lack of harbours, could make such voyages hazardous in the extreme.

Given a sufficient craft and knowing his destination, an early navigator might have preferred to give the immediate vicinity of the islands a wide berth. Therefore, we have no right to assume that Orkney was a stepping-stone to Shetland from the south, or that the converse occurred in Shetland when the Norse invasion took place in turn. So let us look at longer journeys. To Caithness is roughly 100 miles, and to Rattray Head in Aberdeen 135. From the west of Scotland the distances are greater; Cape Wrath being 156 miles and Lewis 180. To Norway the Bergen approaches are also 180, and the Naze of Norway 287. Faroe is actually nearer than either the Hebrides or Norway, but the 176 miles which separate it from Iceland were such impediments to early navigation that the difference is time of settlement may be as much as 2,500 years.

People who live by the sea are apt to exploit her resources for generations and then turn their back on her. This is well exemplified through all Shetland's history. When they do exploit her, it may lead them far afield; to Greenland and Faroe in one generation, to South Georgia or Vancouver or New Zealand in another. A static period, when even shore fishing is hardly indulged in, may be followed by one of intense activity. Although lands separated by water may lie quite near to one another, there must be strong incentives for fishing and trade, let alone settlement. Shetland's connection with Norway, for example, was a reversal of her historical system of communications, which lasted for 800 years in actuality, and by repeopling the islands, is bound to have its effects for as many centuries more.

In the centuries before Christ we are not concerned with Norway. Its archaeology is entirely different from that of Shetland. But we may well ask ourselves what it was that brought primitive settlers to Shetland. There were certain quite definite advantages. No trees required to be cut down and there was sufficient pasture for stock. Peat could be used as fuel, and was so widely used that the double and sometimes treble walls of the earliest dwellings are often cavity walls filled with peat-ash. So much for the story of Torf-Einar. If summer was cool, winter was not cold, and there were no long periods of snow. Barley could be grown easily and food could be obtained from the sea and the seashore. There was no wild animals to contend with and the fowl in abundance. Even before the use of textiles, there were sealskins and sheepskins for clothing.

In covering long periods of history we must speculate about changes in climate. Did strong winds always destroy the growing points of trees, as they do now? From the evidence of peat cutting there may have been small copses of birch and willow in very early times, but these were quickly destroyed by human agency and domestic animals.

Shetland owes her boisterous and changeable weather to lying on the line where polar air and the warm south-westerly air stream most frequently meet and where cyclonic storms or depressions have their origin. We are familiar with the difference in weather when the line of depressions is passing far north, as in the summers of 1947 or 1955, or the cool drier conditions when they are farther south. There is a possibility that this line of depressions may not at times in history have passed through Shetland. Thus it is surmised that the weather in the Early Bronze Age and the Viking Period may have been warmer and more settled in summer and cooler and drier in winter, while the four centuries to 400 AD were progressively wetter and more inclement.

These findings, which are indicative rather than convincing, have been arrived at mainly by pollen analysis. By examining microscopically peat or earth which belongs to a certain period, one can find what plants were growing at that time, and deduce the weather from the nature and number of the various grains of pollen. But no pollen analysis from Shetland has been attempted in spite of the official excavations made, and Shetland lying climatically in a critical position on the map, may have been different. There is no likelihood of any extremes of cold, heat, rain, drought, storm or sunshine greater than we have had in our lifetime, but a long-continued spell for generations of excessively rainy weather, say, might have made a considerable difference to the conditions of life.

There have been no Ice Ages since Shetland was first inhabited, as the unexplained, or over-explained, causes of these operate over many thousands of years. But there is a smaller change every 1,600 years which has had its effect both on the climate and the surrounding sea. Once in that period the earth is at its nearest to the sun and the moon to the earth, while both are placed so as to cause the maximum tides in the sea, and a corresponding effect on the atmosphere. This occurred in 1433, and it must also have happened in the 2nd Century BC and about 1,800 BC, if Shetland had any inhabitants then. The tides of the 15th Century caused the migration of herrings from the Baltic to the North Sea and completed the Zuyder Zee. The same century was a time of "exceedingly prevalent poverty" in Orkney. But it must be remembered that we have had extremes in our own day which have exceeded these long-operating factors; for instance the great gale of February 1900, levelled Brochs which had stood for 1.800 years. The fact that the land in Shetland is gradually sinking has had a minor effect in creating new islets, and burying sites beneath the sea; for example, the Brochs at Orbister in Northmavine and Uyeasound.

Much more important from the human point of view were the periodical diseases, the smallpox which swept Shetland every twenty years or so, and the occasional plague, like the Black Death, which no doubt killed one person out of two or three, as it did in Scotland and Norway, and affected the whole land for generations afterwards.

Absolute dating of ancient sites is now possible, but so new that professional archaeologists have hardly used it, either in Shetland or anywhere else. Naturally occurring carbon, such as wood, charcoal, bones of humans and animal grains, etc., contains minute quantities of radioactive carbon, the amount of which declines at a given rate with its age. By measuring the degree of radioactivity remaining it is possible to find the date for when the human or animal or plant was alive. Stonehenge, for example, was in being 3,800 years ago. As there is hardly any ruin among the thousands of Shetland where a little digging will not reveal some bone or charred wood, it is quite possible to give an accurate date now to the types of remains which are mentioned afterwards.

In the meantime we have to rely on changes in the ways of doing things; different ways, for example, of constructing a grave, making and decorating pottery, or making weapons or ornaments. This leaves a great deal of guesswork as to how long people who had an easily recognised system of doing something would take to travel from one place to another, measuring the time in generations or centuries. The road to Shetland is the sea, which is free to all men who have the necessary ships to sail in it, and a man can travel in a ship, no matter how primitive, much easier and farther and faster than he can on foot. It is therefore possible that there were settlers in Shetland much earlier than in some inland parts of Britain, for forests and marshes can make a place less accessible than the sea does.

Although we cannot give a single accurate date, we can say that the earliest remains in Shetland present a more complete picture of the inhabitants than anywhere else in Britain, for there are tombs, temples, houses, fields, walls, stone implements; the complete Neolithic economy in fact, except for the boats that brought them.

The tombs were recognised about twenty years ago. They are found nowhere else but in Shetland. In ground plan, a Neolithic tomb is shaped like a heel of a boot; occasionally like a cocked hat; sometimes square. From the middle of the instep of the heel a passage leads into the centre, ending in a chamber like the arms and head of a very short squat cross, or to put it otherwise, an ace of clubs whose "pips" are square instead of being clover-shaped. Indeed passage and chamber look very like a cross. Surrounding the chamber inside the material of the cairn, like an old type revolving rubber heel in plan, is an inner ring of stone. This might have been the foundation of the cairn proper, which rose over the chamber like a hemispherical dome, the heel shape being the platform and the "instep" a façade with the entrance in the middle.

It is assumed that these earliest tombs were communal burial places, but so far only one or two of have been examined and no remains have been found inside them. One at Pettigersfield, Whalsay, that I excavated twenty years ago was square in outside plan and had a mathematically accurate trefoil chamber that contained some disintegrated pottery, ashes, and vivianite (iron phosphate). The latter indicates bones, while ashes may not point to cremation but to fires lighted in the tomb on the occasion of a fresh burial.

In plan these Shetland Neolithic graves differ so much from those of Orkney that we are forced to conclude they were made by a different people. Orkney graves are massive affairs, with a great variety of forms, so much so that the islands must have been a meeting place for people of widely different traditions and beliefs. But there is no sign that any of this traffic found its way to Shetland. There are no Orkney cairns in Shetland, and there are no heel-shaped or square cairns in Orkney and no trefoil chambers. Orkney resembles Caithness; for resemblances to Shetland we have to go to northern Connaught and Leinster in Ireland, where some of the typical trefoil chambers of Shetland can be exactly paralleled. Unfortunately, we know more about the Shetland cairns than about their prototypes, but the indications are that the first colonists may have come by sea via Ireland and missed Orkney altogether.

It is unfortunate that the only record we have of the antiquities of Shetland, the Inventory of the Royal Commission on Ancient Monuments, is not nearly as exhaustive as that of Orkney. Quite clearly a great deal of ground was not covered, and some of the monuments listed can hardly have been visited, so imperfectly are they described. The numerous house sites, though perfectly familiar to Shetlanders for what they are, being on low ground, and exhibiting in many cases quite clearly the form of a house wall, with sometimes an outer boundary wall enclosing a small "toon", are commonly described in the Inventory as "cairns" if mentioned at all. In fact, though published only in 1946, and in its contents only about ten years older, the Inventory is completed outdated.

If enough is exposed it is quite easy to distinguish burial cairns from houses, though both are naturally found most often now in uncultivated land for cairns are nearly always on hilltops or exposed hill shoulders, while houses are naturally in sheltered places. Remains on low ground, which form an oval ring rather than a mound, are likely to be houses. The matter is usually settled by the finding of stone implements or parts of querns, which occur on every house site.

The houses themselves are quite distinctive. The general shape is oval, or oval with a concave front like a shallow bite taken out of one end. The size varies from thirty up to sixty feet over the long axis. There are two skin walls, an inside and an outside, and the space between is filled with rubble, ashes, or earth, giving a wall six to twelve feet thick. Sometimes in the middle of this infilling there is a third wall with infilling in the spaces between. The inside skin of the house is not oval, but scalloped to as to give deep recesses into the surrounding thick wall infilling. If we compare the inside plan of the building to a human trunk, we usually have one recess for the head, one for each shoulder, and one for each hip. Another comparison could be to an ace of clubs with two extra pips added below, to give five instead of three. The recesses, however, are irregular in shape, sometimes with squared corners, and sometimes approaching one another so closely that they look as if partitioned off from one another.

It is usual to call a house like this a courtyard house, from the idea that the recesses alone were roofed and the middle left uncovered. There is, however, no reason to believe that the Shetland houses were unroofed.

Inside the house there are often drains, and the site may be on a sloping piece of ground which has been partly hollowed out for the foundations. Peat was used for firing, and fires were invariably found, but much of this may not be original, as the houses were reoccupied for many centuries. Steatite (or "kleeber", "klemmel", talc, soapstone) was used commonly to make pots and also to mix with clay for pots. Pumice stone, which drifts ashore so commonly from West Indian or perhaps Icelandic volcanoes, was used to sharpen bone points, although generally all bone has decayed. Quartz was used for scrapers instead of flint, and pecked into rough balls big enough to hold in the hand. These may have been used to fabricate other tools or to work skins. Scoop-shaped querns were used with rubbing stones, which are easily recognised from being flattened on one site. Their favourite implement (1,800 were found at Pettigersfield, Whalsay) was a thin stone, some seven or eight inches long by three to four wide. It was roughly squared at the end and chipped at all the edges, and seems to have been a type of hand hoe. Using a convenient stone as fabricator, I have made one in half an hour. Heavier boat-shaped stones and stubby hammer stones are fairly common. A puzzling implement, very common in Shetland, was of sandstone, shaped rather like a straight, blunt ox horn worn away on one side. This may have been used in wet moor to take peat for fuel, as a chipped implement would be at a disadvantage because of the rootlets in the moor.

Only one whorl, to indicate spinning and cloth making has been found in these houses, and this probably was from a later date. But they intimated the earliest type of Bronze axe (1,500 BC) in stone, and also little socketed hammers. There is nothing at all yet to connect them with the "celt", the beautifully polished smooth axe, or with the Shetland knife, a polished, slate-thin oval stone with a sharp cutting edge. These exotics were probably manufactured in Northmaven, where the stone is found. But a peculiar Whalsay find was oval discs of steatite with a groove round the edge, similar to those used in living memory to stop the legs of sheepskin buoys. There is little doubt that here we have something connected with a leather "bottle".

These people, living entirely in Stone Age conditions, were far from savages. Their houses were dry and comfortable, and probably as snug and roomy as a thatched cottage. In choosing their house sites, they studied shelter from the weather and exposure to the sun. They had their fields and animals and must have noted the passing seasons for their agriculture.

There is no question at all that they grew grain. At Gruting, in a house excavated by Mr Calder, no less than thirty pounds of bere was recovered from among the ashes in the walls, along with the trough quern on which it has been ground. In Whalsay, 35 parts of quern were found and there was abundant vivianite, an iron phosphate which is limy in wet soil, but turns bright green on exposure to air. From this, we can infer a flesh diet, with plenty of bones lying about. From the later sites at Jarlshof, we know that hey had cattle, sheep, pigs, ponies and dogs, but at this early period they did not use shellfish. When we consider how little is left to indicate the fishing activities of a few generations back, we cannot really assume that they were not enriching their lives from the sea as well as the land.

Of the sixty or seventy house sites already known, those at Gruting and Pettigersfield, Whalsay, have been in part excavated. The Whalsay site is much more compact, with its house, graves on the hill above, and temple. The Gruting sites from Stanydale to Sefster to the Ness of Gruting, are much more scattered and were better peopled. In fact, it may well be that the first inhabitants made a landfall at the Westside. If the identification of Stanydale, and Yuxie in Whalsay as temples is correct, they took their religion with them, and it had come from as far afield as Malta, for these buildings, and in fact some of the houses, are practically duplicated there. Their religion was evidently of great importance in their lives, but what form it took we have no means of knowing.

Every Shetlander is familiar with the walls which cross his hillsides in all directions. If straight, they are probably not more than a century old. Older walling has numerous bends. Such walls were completed in turf on a stone foundation. A turf wall offered so much resistance to a cross wind that it might be blown down for its full length in a storm. The bends prevented this. Holes might be blown in the wall but the main structure was saved. Some of these older walls are Norse scattald (or common) divisions. Fetlar, for example, had ten scattalds and Unst 21, and these were fiscal and defence units. Often we have a wall in the common which form an enclosure on itself or with the shoreline. This may be a pund, or piece of common appropriated in Norse times to private or communal uses, for example, the rounding up of ewes for milking. But if there is a sign of an oval building inside, it is almost certainly a croft of Stone or Bronze Age times. Similarly every Shetlander is familiar with the wall which appears when three or four feet or peat have been removed, and we must ascribe this too to these early times.

Jarlshof begins where these early settlements leave off. The Bronze Age houses are of the same general plan, but smaller. Shellfish, absent before, are now consumed in great numbers, and animals seem now to be more important than cereal growing. But these later people collected manure for their fields, the oldest instance of its use in Britain, just as the Gruting bere, mentioned before, is the earliest known cereal in the north of Europe.

It is now time to go back to pick up the burial record, for fashions in this changed. Fragments of beakers, a short squat pottery tumbler belonging to the first stage of the Bronze Age, have been found in at least three places in Shetland, twice in a cist. A cist may be described as a box made of upright stones buried in the ground, with a bottom sometimes of stone and sometimes of clay. It was covered with a heavy capstone or lid, and in Shetland measured over four feet in length by two in breadth. From outside examples we know that the body was laid on its side with the knees drawn up.

Cist graves must have been very common in Shetland. The earliest cists are found in heel shaped cairns, and in the case of the Whalsay site before mentioned the cairn covering a cist is only thirty feet from that covering a trefoil chambered tomb, a sign that the incomers had probably mingled freely with their predecessors. But normally the cairn over a cist was round. Large cairns are particularly common on the Westside of Shetland, but the cist graves, although great collections of stone, were rather structureless compared with the earlier tombs. Later cists had very small cairns, or none at all, while some have been found in mounds of earth. After a time burial gave way to cremation. In Orkney there are very small cists full of burnt material, but these are rarely recorded from Shetland. Nor is there the series of Bronze Age urns found on the mainland of Britain. Instead we find the ashes in soapstone urns, which were made in Shetland, where the material occurs, and exported also to Orkney. A few ornamented clay urns, unlike the mainland ones, have also been found. With cremation, it is no longer profitable to try to follow the burial record.

In the Bronze Age, we find another typical Shetland mound coming into use for a very different purpose. These "burnt mounds", as they are called, are found beside water, and look like a little green knoll with a crescentic hollow in one side. They are usually full of burnt stones, which are supposed to have been heated and then used in primitive ovens. Baking is still done in this way in Palestine. Probably these mounds were in use for a long time, for the Norse used heated stones in their bath-houses. They do not occur, however, in Norway. There are few Shetland "toons" that do not have these burnt mounds, and they are, unlike the relics so far mentioned, rarely found outside present-day cultivation. But urns have been occasionally found in them.

In Jarlshof there is no sign of bronze at first, but in later houses abundant clay casts were found, both of swords and axes, or late Irish type. In making the weapons, the clay moulds had to be broken, and Jarlshof furnished the first complete evidence of how these weapons were made. That the Jarlshof smith was the only one ever to set up in Shetland is very unlikely; there are records of knives, spears and swords elsewhere, and a year or two ago I was shown a bronze pin, with the information that it was an implement used to trim the wick of a candle!

A century or two before the birth of Christ the first people using iron arrived, and they seem to have come in numbers, and were, quite possibly, refugees. At Jarlshof they built round houses over twenty feet across, with a central hearth and radial partitions from the inner walls to give cubicles, each of which might have its own fire. But they seem at the same time to have occupied the ruins of dwellings wherever these were available, for their pottery, with its steatite tempering, flattened and flanged rims, and grass-tempering is found on sites which were already centuries old and probably long abandoned. They brought with them, too, the making of souterrains, under-ground tunnels which were probably used as storehouses, a purpose which they must have served pretty ineffectually in Shetland's damp climate. These were in use for a long time.

The newcomers arrived at a critical period. The age of iron brought with it new weapons, and when men have new weapons they will group together and fight, as they did after the invention of gunpowder, as they have done in our day after the discovering of high explosive, and as they will, unless God helps us, after the invention of the uranium and hydrogen bombs.

Groups of men will also, if they can get away with it, enrich themselves form the labour of others, and use whatever superior means they can command to do so. If they cannot employ them, they will make them slaves. So the Iron Age became really an age of iron, with slavery as a motive and war as a means to drive men to action.

At first the islands were left alone, escaping the spate of hill forts which began to appear in Scotland. But in time the tentacles of Rome reached out towards Britain, the supply of slave prisoners of war diminished as there were fewer enemies left to fight, and the refugees in the islands became the target of slave traders. It was then, under the most extraordinary social system that the islands ever possessed, that the brochs were built.

HOLED STONES — HOES, LOOM WEIGHTS, SINKERS, ETC.

RUDE IMPLEMENTS

Chapter 2

The Brochs and After

THE five hundred brochs in the world have their maximum density in Shetland, Orkney and Caithness and terminate in Sutherland. There are a few coastal sites on the west coast, more in the Western Isles and Skye and about half-a-dozen isolated examples in lowland and south Scotland. It would probably be true that they originated in Orkney or Caithness, and from Orkney spread to Shetland and down the west coast. The few in south Scotland may represent small bands of settlers from the north, and it is interesting that one of their brochs was destroyed by the Romans.

The brochs are unique in many ways. They are the most complicated drystone structure ever made. They conform closely to a general pattern, as if they had all been built to order within a short time. They appear to have had a short life; in fact, it might be legitimate to infer that some were never finished. They point to an organised life, perhaps on a semi-military basis, in the north, such as had never existed before, and never has since.

Some present-day houses have three rooms, some four or five. Broch differences were of that nature, and there were walled headlands and loch defences which were not brochs at all, but belong to the same period. But Mousa, which is the only broch nearly complete, can be taken as a sample of all.

In a typical broch a circular area, 20 to 35 feet in diameter, was surrounded by a wall 10 to 15 feet thick and a dozen feet or more in height. The only entrance from the outside was a passage less than three feet wide and five feet or so in height. This passage had checks for one or two doors. Built in the thickness of the wall were chambers, rather in the shape of a tea-cosy, a dozen feet or more in length, and as high and wide as the wall would permit. These chambers were roofed by corbelling, that is, laying each course of stones a little farther in until the top could be closed by a single slab. Corbelling differs from arch-making. There are no keystones. All the stones are laid flat, and are held in position by pressure from above and from the sides. The doors of these chambers were low openings in the side and led into the interior of the broch. Sometimes there were guard chambers on one or both sides of the entrance passage with an opening through which spears could be thrust and occasionally there were gaps between the passage lintels through which an unwanted guest might be assailed from above. A quarter of the distance round the left inside wall of the broch an opening led into a chamber, from the right side of which a stair started to climb spirally half round the building until it reached the top.

Except for the wall chambers, the stair opening and the entrance passage, the lower part of the broch wall was solid up to about a dozen feet. From that height there was a double circular wall, outside and inside, with a passage between through which a man might walk crouching. This passage was roofed with heavy stone lintels at the height of five or six feet, and formed a circular tunnel round the broch inside its wall, which was only interrupted by its stairway. One could spring across from the stair into this gallery and make a circuit inside the wall of the broch until he came to a dead end behind the stair. The double wall was continued upwards in another gallery, the lintels of one forming the floor of the one above. Mousa, a small broch, is 43 feet high; bigger examples might be sixty feet high, sufficient for seven or eight galleries.

The wall galleries were partly lit by ladder-like rows of openings in the inside of the broch. These windows usually started above a lintel of the door into one of the "tea-cosy" chambers in the base, so relieving pressure on it, but their main purpose seems to have been to make the inner wall less rigid, so that as the building settled the lintels of the galleries should remain horizontal. Also for stability the outer wall was built with a batter, or inward slope of about 1 foot in 10 of height. This was achieved by setting each course or stonework a little farther in, and may be seen to perfection at Jarlshof. In addition the outer side of the double gallery wall was usually thicker than the inner. Even so, most brochs have collapsed by the sagging f the outside wall. The galleries themselves enabled a high wall to be made without the use of staging.

Many, but not all, brochs had a position of great natural strength, and even here walls were added. These ranged from an outer circular wall in the case of Mousa, Culswick, Underhoull and others, to much more complicated defences.

The labour force required to assemble and construct a broch would probably be in the nature of 100 men working for a year. This leaves out of account the expenditure of time and energy in quarrying, rough-dressing and transporting the stones. Mousa, now uninhabited, had 11 households at the end of the 18th century, say a maximum of 25 to 30 men. It is very unlikely to have had more at any time, and this broch, like numerous others on outer points of land, must have been built by people who lived some distance away, in this case on the mainland opposite.

Shetland at its best had two feudal castles, and all the local lairds of later times (very small fry indeed) would not have added up to a fraction of her hundred brochs, so it is useless to think of a lord controlling a group of serfs. From the position of the brochs we can hardly think of families living under the shadow of the broch walls. If we think of pirate lairs we are bound to ask, "Piracy against whom?" Besides, brochs are not often convenient to harbours. We have a form of life based on a group much larger than the family, and a communal effort to meet some unprecedented sort of danger.

It is usual to speak as if all the defensive sites in Shetland and Orkney were brochs, but there are defences in lochs and on headlands which were quite different. The original defence in Clickimin, Sumburgh Head, the Blue Mull in Unst, Strandibroch in Fetlar, Huxter Loch in Whalsay, the Ness of Burgi in Scatness, the Holm of Califf and Brindister Loch are cases in point. In Huxter and Scatness a section of true broch walling was apparently added to an original fort, and in Clickimin the Iron Age A people who built the round huts at Jarlshof had occupied the islet before the broch was built. In the Hebrides, there are many loch duns, some of which may be early, and few real brochs. This may be explained if these islands were harried earlier and to a greater extent.

The close adherence of the brochs to a single plan suggests that they were all built about the same time. The Norman square tower keeps, for example, were all built within fifty years, and were quite different from the mote and bailey castles which preceded them. Brochs were built by outsiders, as we know from the skill of their construction, co-operating with the local inhabitants, as we deduce from the amount of labour required. As far as Shetland is concerned, we know that the outsiders came from Orkney, for we find both local pottery and that of the newcomers. And from particular finds, such as bone dice, handled bone weaving combs, special bone bobbins and crucibles for metal working, we assume that there was a connection which leads us as far afield as south-west England, and thence to Western France.

It seems reasonable, then, to assume that the broch builders came by the western route in considerable numbers and settled in north Scotland. This suggests that they were refugees. A likely time for such a migration was 56BC, a year before Caesar's visit to Britain, when he overcame the Venti. This tribe held Brittany, and were skilled seamen who commanded the mouth of the English Channel. Caesar tells us they were expert slingers. Probably other people from Western France tried to get well out of Roman reach at the time, moving by the old route along the western seaboard. Perhaps there had already been tentative slave raiding along this route; when in the latter half of the first century AD it became an organised business, the new colonists had to organise in self-defence.

Their chief weapons were spears and slings. A defended island or headland was merely a place of refuge, where they had no chance of hitting back, and in particular, no extra shelter for women and children. In Caithness and Orkney, where the brochs first were made, there were few of either defensible headlands or lake islets.

In choosing sites the main factors were defence, proximity to fresh water, the possibility of signalling to other brochs by smoke or fire, seaward view, the command of navigable channels, and the command of harbours. Brochs themselves were usually not sited on harbours. To attack them an enemy had to leave his ships and run the risk of being cut off. Those who know the Shetland broch sites will realise how well these conditions are fulfilled.

Apart from the months of June, July and August, there was little fear of attack, and for the rest of the year many of the Shetland brochs were probably not manned.

We are not without evidence of the value of a broch as a means of defence. About 1155 Mousa, smallest and perhaps most weakly situated of all the Shetland brochs, venerable and perhaps a little ruinous, was besieged by no less a person than the Earl of Orkney, who could command fifteen dragon ships, and who on this occasion probably summoned all the forces he could muster. For he was going, against that lady's will, the save the honour of his mother. This fickle dame, already a widow, had run off with a Shetlander, Erlend the Young, and they had taken refuge in the castle. The stronghold could not be taken, so Earl Harald settled down to a siege, which was equally unavailing. Finally the Earl had to endure what he could not cure, and approve the new family alliance.

The primary danger in Shetland was from the south, and we have a dozen brochs, including Jarlshof, commanding every voe and inlet where shelter could be found. Mousa and Burland guard the sound there. Three brochs commanded Lerwick harbour; four hampered passage by the other side of Bressay. The Nesting voes were studded with brochs; two commanded the only anchorages in Whalsay. The North Isles anchorages had nine towers, and another nine dominated the sounds of Yell, Unst and Fetlar.

On the west side of the Mainland the story is similar. Wherever there is sheltered water there is a broch not far away. The watch-tower of Culswick commanded all the sea to the south-west, just as Sae Breck in Eshaness kept watch over St. Magnus Bay. Where transit from coast to coast is easy, brochs tend to cluster. There are six from Voe to Scousburgh in Dunrossness. The passage at Quarff had two brochs in close proximity at its east end, and four in Burra and Trondra at its west, which at the same time denied the harbour at Scalloway to the enemy. East Houlland guards the route from Aith Voe to Bixter Voe; three guarded the narrows between St. Magnus Bay and Sullom Voe; Windhouse watched the "waist" of Yell.

A few inland sites in lochs may not have been brochs in the sense of towers, and some, which may have been refuges for women and children, were paired with fighting brochs in close proximity. Such pairs are Burravoe and Loch of Kettlester (Yell), Symbister and Loch of Huxter (Whalsay), Vidlin and Burga Water (Lunnasting), Benston and Loch of Benston (Nesting) and Lunabister and Loch of Broo (Dunrossness).

It is clear that maritime attack from the south was feared. There is no accident in the sites chosen. Brough in Burra had an uninterrupted view of the east sea through the Quarff gap; Brough in Whalsay could spread an alarm to the whole North Isles; Underhoull in Unst was in sight of at least six other brochs and so the tale goes on, in Orkney as well as in Shetland.

One thing is certain, that the broch-builders had no need to defend themselves against the original inhabitants. Nor does it seem that that was the case with the few brochs which we find in southern Scotland, very few indeed, as if small groups had wandered far afield, and taken their style of building with them. At Torwoodlee in Selkirkshire there was one broch of a pair. It was complete in the first century, and had stood long enough to be torn down, apparently by the Romans. It is worth noting that the Veneti, from the same area of France established themselves on a friendly basis among the tribes of Wessex. Whether pressure of population compelled the broch people to move in such a way down into Scotland we do not know. The hill forts there were already old, as in the main they seem to have been built by the first Iron Age invaders three or four centuries before. The name Pict was first used by the Roman writer Euminius in 297, when these were fighting the Romans in northern England, and the Venerable Bede (673-735) tells us that the Picts first came to Ireland, where they received no welcome, and then went and settled in the northern parts of Britain. Bede lived at Jarrow on Tyne. Nennius (c. 850) is much more definite. He says that the Picts occupied the Orkneys, and from these islands wasted many districts. Finally they settled in the northern part of Britain, and held the third part of the island when Nennius wrote. The mass of references in between to the Picts do nothing to lead us to the broch builders of nine centuries before, who may well have been the original Picts.

The broch-builders were farmers, fishermen, stock-breeders, fowlers, hunters and beachcombers. They probably had to be. The broch midden at West Burra in 1951 included forty-foot whale, common and grey seal, red-deer, pony, cattle, sheep (two breeds, one goat-like), pigs of all sizes, some with tusks up to four inches long, swan, gannet, cormorant, raven, gull, cod, oyster, mussel, limpet, whelk, cockle. From other brochs we can add to their menu grampus, porpoise, dogfish, haddock, crab. They caught the otter, and in Scottish brochs fox, wolf, wild boar and wild cat have been found. They kept the domestic cat, which is said to have been introduced into Britain in Roman times. They ground their oats and barley in querns which were often completely hollowed out, like a "knockin stane", and not the scoop-shaped trough querns of earlier times. At some period they began to use "hand mills" or rotary querns. Where the broch was out-of-the-way we can see the extent of their cultivation, as at Burgan, Gluss or at Brindister. But in many cases the broch is the nucleus from which our present-day "toons" have sprung.

Bone is hard and makes excellent tools. Whale bones were put to various uses, rafters, door-sockets, stools, cups and agricultural implements. Horn was widely used, as nowadays, for tool and knife handles. Bone combs were for ordinary and domestic use (these with the teeth beautifully sawn and often skilfully riveted together). A handled comb, something like an outsize fork, was used to keep the threads parallel on an upright loom. Bone was also utilised for beads, dice, buttons (with metal shanks), pins, pegs, needles, awls, whorls for spinning, tool handles, implements for smoothing, implements for making pottery, and a host of varied uses.

Needles, bodkins and borers for stitching skins have been found, and even a pair of bronze tweezers, supposed to be for pulling the thongs through the holes in sewing. In living memory the Shetland fishermen used to spin "toms" (fine lines for fishing) by twisting horse-hair on a spindle made of a stick stuck into a circular piece of peat. They were using the last degenerate descendant of the spindle and whorl, the only spinning machine Scotland possessed until the spinning wheel ousted it a few centuries ago. Whorls, usually made of soapstone, are common in brochs.

Broch pottery generally was both plain and ornamented, consisting chiefly of unglazed globular vessels, with everted rims and bulging sides. In Shetland there are two kinds, alien and native, representing the incomers from Orkney and the people with whom they mixed. In a number of cases red lustrous Roman ware of the first and second centuries called Samian ware, has been found, in one case in Orkney carefully mended by metal clamps.

Stone was used for querns, lamps, beads, moulds and cups, and stones with holes bored in them have been found, either sinkers for use in fishing or loom weights.

Rings, bracelets, pins, brooches, etc. have been found in bronze, and we know that they were manufactured on the spot, because clay moulds, crucibles with metal fragments, and cakes of the rough metal have been discovered. The bronze ferrule of a spear shaft from Harray, Orkney, has six companions from Antrim.

Iron disintegrates rapidly, but spear-heads, chisels, dagger blades, knives, arrowheads, swords, hatchets and rivets, have been found in fragmentary condition, although not in Shetland. When we consider how rare weapon finds are in medieval castles, we cannot assume that the scarcity of weapon finds indicates a structure primarily defensive. Sling-stones may be found in almost any broch.

Broch-builders were certainly familiar with the warfare of the time. The solid lower wall was proof against battering rams; the height and the ever-present supply of ammunition in the stones of the upper storeys made scaling-ladders useless. The outer defences were of approved military pattern, and required many men to man them; the enemy approaching the doorway had to expose his unshielded right flank, or do something more dangerous if the broch wall was on his left hand. Once crouched in the passage he could, in some brochs, be harassed from guard chambers on the right and left, and between the lintels from above. Inside the broch, he was the target for missiles from the wall-tops and tiers of internal "windows". If he mounted the stairs, which was always entered from the left quadrant of the broch after one had negotiated the passage and got inside, he had again to expose his right side to reach it, and then could not freely use his right arm to fight his way upstairs. The stair steps, besides, were made so short the he could not possibly get a firm footing, and from the gallery ends enthusiasts could prod his back with spears. No wonder Mousa could not be taken by the Orkney earl.

The internal arrangements of the brochs are still not clear, as the modern excavations have preserved internal features which were constructed by people who tore down the brochs when they were no longer needed for defence and lived in them. A primary feature was that the inside wall went up straight for several feet, and then was set in a few inches, forming a ledge or scarcement round the broch. There might be two or three of these in the height. A use may have been as ledges to support lofts or an inside verandah roof. Probably they were also constructional to give equal balance in the sides of the wall galleries. The outside wall was set in an inch or two at the foundations after every course of stonework, but after it had reached a height of perhaps a dozen feet it went practically straight up. The inner wall was vertical for perhaps the same distance; then it was set back by the width of the scarcement.

How the brochs were roofed is doubtful. A leather awning stretched over the top is possible, as in Roman times leather was widely used for military purposes, but it would have left the inside in darkness when in use. Post holes inside some brochs seem to suggest that there was a circular verandah inside supported on the lower scarcement, leaving the centre of the broch open for fires. A well or tank for water was a feature of most brochs. Possibly the roofing arrangements in winter and summer would have differed.

It is easier to guess why the broch came into being than how. Anyone seeing the nuraghs of Sardinia, which are rather smaller towers in similar positions, and are certainly older than the brochs, could get from these the idea of the tower shape, the long entrance passage, the staircase in the wall and the corbelled chambers built in the wall thickness. Indeed, a friend of mine who served for two months in a nuragh during the war, and who has seen pictures of brochs and their outer constructions, regards the two as closely related. But the broch has many features of its own. The lintelled hollow upper walls, and the open centre are features which belong to the broch alone. If among the refugees who colonised the islands there were some who had seen service in Sardinia with the Roman army, they might have attempted a similar type of defence. Sandstone slabs are abundant in Caithness and Orkney, and lintelling presented no problem. The confined space of a nuragh may have suggested a larger structure, which made an open centre are the two vital differences between broch and nuragh.

The popular theory at present, put forward it must be said by archaeologists who have had little first hand acquaintance with brochs, is that they were a variety of buildings, merging on the one hand into the broch tower, and on the other into the round house or Cornwall, the wag of Caithness, the earth house of the Hebrides, and nebulous forms constructed in timber. Most of them were defended farmhouses about eight feet high. This ignores galleries, chambers, staircases and all typical features, is contrary to widespread local records that towers did exist, and conjures up a fantastically thick, indefensible wall, with purposeless chambers, and stairs leading nowhere, topped by a ridiculously flimsy roof. To anyone acquainted with island brochs it is simply nonsensical.

An older theory, suggested by the Royal Commission on Ancient Monuments, is that the brochs evolved from the double walls defending the necks of promontories, which were gradually enclosed on themselves to defend first an irregular and then a round area, after which the builders began to plan for height. The weakness is that there are no buildings where we can trace the steps of such a complicated development, and we are left to infer that corbelled chambers and tower both grew of their own accord. The length of time required for such a development is too great.

The broch towers lasted for only a short period. The design was very quickly perfected and they fell into disuse as soon as the immediate danger was past. In Jarlshof the broch was abandoned soon after its completion, and a section of its defences was torn down to provide building stone.

If we accept what little evidence there is to connect the broch-builders with western France as valid, and make the best of the traditions about the Picts, we have the following sequence. A group of people, with a limited contact with Roman civilisation, scatter as refugees before the Romans at the time of the invasion of Gaul, discarding most of their native culture on the way. As a mixed race, they evolve the broch in Orkney (probably) and in Caithness as a means of defence against slaving fleets. The broch spreads to Shetland, and later to the Hebrides. The intensive occupation corresponds to the Roman interest in Scotland; roughly the century from the time of Agricola. With the decline of Roman power broch-building quickly loses its urgency, and many of the builders migrate southwards.

While the brochs were short-lived as defences, most of them lasted for a long time as dwellings. Nearly every Shetland broch which has been excavated has the same features, the inside has been converted into a wheelhouse. A wheelhouse is in plan like a very rough wheel with the hub cut out. How many compartments it has depends on the "spoke walls", but the least is three. Where the hub is situated there was a central fireplace. The spoke walls were gradually made wider upwards until they met, giving a number of stone roofed recesses, with the communal fire in the middle, open perhaps to the sky. Sometimes there were doors at the wide end of the cubicles next the circular wall, and these communicated from one cubicle to another. At Jarlshof there are two outside wheelhouses built partly on the outer wall of the broch, and a third built in its inside. The wheelhouse folk often found the inside diameter of the broch too wide for their purpose, and then they built a retaining wall against the inside before putting in their "spokes".

Like that of a mansion divided into flats, the broch masonry is superior to the wheelhouses. But from the point of view of human activity, the flats may be the more useful of the two. The wheelhouses lasted for many peaceful centuries. Outhouses and dwellings were erected and pulled down and re-erected in the vicinity of the brochs, their defences were broken into, and their upper stones utilised. Thus the brochs did, in fact, become farmhouses.

Wheelhouses are found in groups in the Hebrides, and there may have been a certain amount of migration from there, as a new pottery is in use and also the rotary quern (hand-mill) supplementing the earlier hollowed-out type. This migration may have happened between the second and third centuries AD but any attempt to separate the broch and wheelhouse people must depend on the thorough scientific excavation of one or two untouched brochs, which Jarlshof and Clickimin were not. At present any find in a broch may apply equally to the later wheelhouses, and it is quite possible that the sites were inhabited continuously down to 800AD when the Norse put in an appearance.

Historical references in early times are invariably to Orkney. The first definite reference to Shetland is the remark that Thule was seen by Agricola's fleet when it went round Britain. St. Serf and St. Kentigern are both said to have brought Christianity to Orkney, and St. Cormac is said to have visited Orkney in the sixth century. It is probably that Shetland was not left out by these determined evangelists. St. Colme is given in a 16th century reference to Cunningsburgh, and St. Ninian is commemorated in St. Ninian's Isle, and these are the only definite names pointing to the Celtic church. But we have the three islands of Papa Stour, Papa Little and Papa at Burra and the place-name Papil (priest's dwelling) at Yell, Unst, Fetlar and Burra, and "papa" in Old Norse signified an Irish priest. A very interesting fact is that Ogam writing, an Irish form of writing of which there are only 15 examples on the Mainland of Scotland and two in Orkney, has been discovered seven or eight times in Shetland, three times at St. Ninian's Isle, twice at Cunningsburgh, once at Bressay and Lunnasting, and once at Whalsay. Only two of the Pictish symbols, so common in north-east Scotland, are known, one at Sandness, now lost, and a disc found at Jarlshof; but at least ten stones or fragments with Irish ornament exist. Five of these are from Papil in Burra, three being in the County Buildings, one with a plain cross still at Papil, and the other in the National Museum in Edinburgh. In addition a rune fragment reading "raised a stone" (a grave-stone formula) was discovered there in 1952. How many more stones may lie in the old graveyard of Papil no one can say. The present ruined church, abandoned in 1920, was built from the ruins of a 12th century towered church, like that of Egilsey in Orkney, which again replaced and earlier building. There were two other towered churches in Shetland, at Ireland, Dunrossness, and Tingwall, and outside these Shetland churches and two in Orkney, all the rest of the type are found in East Anglia.

From comparing the designs on the Papil stones with Irish relics, they may be dated to the 8th and 9th centuries, while an interlaced cross from Papil and another from St. Ola's Church, Kirkhouse, Whiteness, are Irish 10th century work. The Papil rune stone is 11th century. As the three latter centuries were those of the Viking raids, and as the rune stone found at Papil marks a Norse burial, we must assume that the Papil site has remained sacred until our own heathen days, for except for the graveyard, it has now been abandoned for 36 years. There seems no reason to doubt now about the Irish monks who sought far-away places like Faroe and Iceland before the Norse. The Papil monks were definitely Irish. That they were able to keep their community going during the invasions can be surmised from the fortune of one of their mother churches, Clonmacnios in Ireland. In the ninth and tenth centuries it was sacked three times by the Irish, twice by the Danes, and once by the two combined. Yet this was the period of its greatest artistic magnificence. Forty-five out of 117 crosses in the Isle of Man are Scandinavian, and the Bressay Stone, now in the National Museum, almost certainly is. And the first stone found at Papil (in 1877) has a lower panel added to it by a Norse artist, a design, picking at or perhaps whispering to a human head. Many of the Norse settlers in Ireland and Scotland embraced Christianity very early, certainly much earlier than 995, the date of the official conversion of Earl Sigurd Hlodverson of Orkney by the Norwegian king, Olaf Tryggvason, who adopted the simple expedient of seizing and threatening to kill the Earl's son, and then carrying the boy off as a hostage lest his father should waver in faith.

At Mail, Cunningsburgh, four fragments of stone with Ogam writing and three stones with runes have been found where the ancient chapel once stood, another testimony to an Irish sacred site which became Norse. At the Cross Kirk ruin at Breckon, Eshaness, a rune stone was found, which is now in private possession. Over ninety churches and chapels are listed by the Royal Commission on Ancient Monuments, but the majority of these are merely sites. In ancient Norse times the whole parishes were divided into scattalds, which paid taxes together and contributed to the common defence in a similar way. Each scattald seems to have had a chapel. The majority of these were from the 11th century onwards, and fell into disuse with the Reformation. The fortunes of the older sites have varied. The only proof of some is the evidence of finds or place-names. In Fetlar, for example, we have Papil Water (now the Loch of Tresta) and the Kloster Dek (or dyke), but the building which gave both their names is not to be seen. The Old Norse word "klaustr" means a convent or cloister. In other cases a graveyard might be added or a new church be built on an older site. In very few cases, however, has all local knowledge been lost of the spot where a sacred building once stood.

CHAPTER 3 _____

The Norse Invasion

ABOUT 1150 years ago Shetland was colonised from Norway, and this caused a great change whose results will be felt, with lessening effect, through many more generations. For the Norse settlement was so overwhelming that all trace of the previous inhabitants was lost. Only in two other parts of their conquered lands did the same thing occur; Orkney, where the Scottish flood began rolling backwards after 600 years, and Lewis, where the Gaels in time swamped the Norse, who have become more Gaelic than the Gaels themselves.

The vital question from a historical standpoint is when the invasion took place. Before examining the evidence we can make two categorical statements, first that the Viking invasion was a complete reversal of all previous movements of peoples, and second that the archaeology of Shetland and Norway before the invasion is quite distinct and unrelated.

Our written records are Irish annals, English chronicles and the sagas of the Norse themselves. Our archaeological records are British finds in Norway and Norse finds in Britain. They are unanimous.

In the days of King Beorhtric of Wessex (786-802) "came first three ships of the Northmen from Haeretha to the king's town, because he knew not what they were; and they slew him; and those were the first ships of Danish men that sought the land of England." So Beaduheard made history by riding to his death from Dorchester to Portland. His visitors were Norwegians from Hordaland, and they had coasted the North Sea.

In 793, the Vikings sacked the church at Lindisfarne, in Northumbria. Alcuin, a scholar at the court of Charlemagne, commented, "It was not thought possible that they could have made such a voyage."

The records are now annual. The Ulster records of 794 record attaches on "all the islands of Britain," and the monasteries of Wearmouth and Jarrow were attacked. "Some of their ships were destroyed by bad weather." In 795 Lambey Island near Dublin was attached, and Wales, Iona and Skye were pillaged. Ireland was again attached in 796, Ulster and Kintyre in 797, Man in 798, Aquitaine in France in 799. For a century the dwellers on the coast or on rivers waited in fear and trembling for the devastation which some high summer was bound to bring.

Warlike plundering by large fleets began in 810 in North Holland, when Godfrey of Denmark warred against Charlemagne with 200 ships. From 819 onwards Ireland was plundered by Norwegian fleets of 60 to 70 ships, which appeared in the Boyne, the Liffey, and at Dublin and Carlingford; in 830 it was Holland's turn again, in 840 France and Germany, and from 850 England.

The settlement phase is recorded as early as 826 in Meath in Ireland. In 835 we hear of Irish plundering on Christmas Day, and in 841 Dublin became a base for the raiders. The Vikings wintered in France at the mouth of the Loire in 836, at the Seine in 851, and in England at Thanet in Kent in 850.

It is against this background that we must place the Norse colonisation of Shetland. The last Irish records are of Pictish expeditions against the Orkneys in 682 and 709, when they may have been debatable land between Picts and Scots. Except for the voyages of Irish monks as far as Faroe in the second quarter of the 8th century, sea travel had been hardly out of sight of land, barring the crossing of the narrowest parts of the North Sea by the Angles. Let us examine the boats available.

A 4th century boat was found buried at Nydam in Jutland in 1863, and is now in Kiel museum. It is 75 feet long, 12 ½ feet beam and 3 ½ deep. Clinker-built of oak, it has a keel plank, and five wide planks on each side, complete except for the two upper strakes, which have a piece added. There are stem and stern posts, ribs and "tafts". The ribs are lashed to cleats on the side planks under the bulwarks. The boards are clenched with iron rivets. The 15 pairs of oars, 12 feet at the longest, were rowed against tholes made fast with rope to the top of the gunwale. The stems project sharply.

The absence of an outside keel made a sail impossible, and gave a weakness owing to the length of the ship which is compensated for by bringing the sides up steeply. This made the boat so "rank" that it must always have been ballasted. The steering, half oar, half rudder, was badly secured on the aft starboard quarter, and the long, narrow vessel must have been awkward both to row and steer. Yet in vessels like this the Saxons harried the Roman shore and later crossed to England. For wider waters it was useless.

The Sutton Hoo "ghost ship" excavated in Suffolk in 1939 was 86 feet long by 14 wide. The wood was away, but every rivet and plank was visible in the sand. It was again mastless, with 19 pairs of oars. There was a keel board, and nine strakes on each side, fastened to the ribs with riveted wooden braces. The date is 650-670.

A vessel with ten pairs of oars and her "fowerereen" were found at Kvalsund, Möre in 1920. She was 59 by 10 by 3 feet. The ribs, like the Hydam ship, are single pieces fastened to cleats on the side planks. The stems are attached to the keel by an overlap with wooden pins. The gunwale, as before, is simply a thickened upper strake. There are eight strakes, each "skaired" in several places. Under waterline the boards are lashed to the ribs; above they are fastened by wooden nails. The rudder is perfectly secured. The keel plank, eight inches wide, has clamps for the ribs, and there is an outer keel four inches high and two thick. the ship is probably 7th century.

Two ships found at Oseberg (840 AD) and Gokstad (850 to 900) on Olso Fjord, date from the peak of viking discovery. The Oseberg ship, 70 feet long and 16 beam, was a sort of yacht, found with rich grave goods, and the skeletons of two women. She was slightly built, with 12 strakes and fifteen pairs of oar-holes just below the gunwale. She could not have made ocean voyages.

A model of the Gokstad vessel crossed the Atlantic in 1893, reaching speeds up to 10 knots. She was 78 feet long (73 waterline) by 16 ½ by 3 ½. Her freeboard amidships was two feet. The keel of 57 feet was extended by deadwood to 65. The 16 side planks were 1 to 1 ½ inches thick by 7 to 9 wide. The was caulked with cows' hairs and pitch. The stem and stern posts were fastened to the keel proper by lashed and nailed immediate pieces.

The stump of the mast was 12 ½ inches thick and it may have been 40 feet long. The yard was 35 feet long, 8 ½ inches diameter at the centre, 3 ½ at the slings. The larges of the 16 pairs of oars was 17 feet, and they fitted through holes in the third strake below the rail. The oar-holes, closed by shutters, consisted of a round hole for the oar, with horizontal side slits for the blade. There was no sign of benches for the rowers, for in large ships the middle was free, and rowers sat on chests or short side benches resting on the ribs. With the ship were three boats, one 25 feet long, which must have been towed astern.

Several ship graves have been found, as at Tune, Ostfold, and Gunnershaug near Bergen, but they add nothing to the above, nor do they clarify what may now be suggested, that up to the first Viking raids the Norwegians had no vessels capable of carrying a force of men to Shetland, that, in fact, up to that time seafaring was a matter of coasting. There is no evidence to suggest otherwise.

Even the viking ships themselves were not very seaworthy. Designed for inshore work in fjord and river mouth, for shallow water and easy beaching, they must have been uncomfortable in the open ocean. The sagas often refer to their unseaworthiness. "You cannot go in longships thither (to Faroe from Iceland), but I will have two merchant ships made ready for you." The tow boats, and the short period of four months at sea are farther evidence of precarious navigation. Of the apparently more seaworthy merchant ship we are once told, "All eighteen men stand baling."

There were no cooking facilities on the viking ships. Cooking pots were carried for the monotonous diet of gruel, meal, butter, salt fish, whey and water, enlivened by ale or the slaughter of occasional stolen animals, but the voyages envisaged were coastal ones and fires, when needed, were lit on shore. Sleeping was under tents.

When cloud hid the sun or the pole star we have remarks like this, "Many lands there are which we might have hit, the Orkneys or Scotland or Ireland." The vessel was actually going from Iceland to Norway.

Sailing depended on a following wind, for the vessels were too long and narrow to tack except in very fine weather. Capes ending in "stad" were turning points where vessels waited for a favourable wind. But without a sail the long viking voyages could never have been undertaken, and a sail implies an outside keel. This was probably the improvement in shipbuilding that made the raids possible.

The Norse invasions covered much wider areas of water than those of the Saxons, but the wider parts of the North Sea were not crossed, and eastern Scotland was left alone. Probably Orkney, with its harbours at Kirkwall and Westray, became a focus for the raiding bands. Perhaps both Shetland and Orkney were over-run between 795 and 820, for the sporadic attacks on Ireland became a yearly occurrence after 819, and the ships must have been then using the northern and western islands as bases. In fact, everything points to the conclusion that the unfortunate generation of Shetlanders born in the first half of the 9th century may have been harried unbearably before permanent settlers came over. Yet, in spite of the absence of Celtic place names, it is impossible to think that the isles could have altogether emptied before the Norse, or that some did not remain to mix with the less aristocratic peasants who formed the first settlements. Probably, from the simultaneous occupation of Orkney, escape was largely cut off.

Dicuil, an Irish monk, writing about 825, mentions islands divided by narrow sounds, abandoned, after being inhabited for over a century by Irish hermits, because of Northern robbers. These, without doubt the Faroes, received their colonisation under Grim Kamban about 860. All the Norse sources place the settlement of the Scottish colonies and also Iceland and Faroe in the reign of Harald Harfagri, and after the battle of Hafrsfjord, when Harfagri overcame the combined forces of his enemies. The year 872 was the date of the colonisation of Iceland, and battle and everything else is dated to this year. Many Norwegian scholars, however, now accept a century-old theory which places Hafrsfjord thirty years later. Whenever it happened, it seems reasonable to suppose that the colonies received an influx of new settlers. But we can be certain that the Scottish islands and Men had been well colonised before Hafrsfjord, and not merely by viking bands. The question is, when?

It must be said categorically that the Vikings are never mentioned in Irish, English or Continental records until shortly before 800, and after that date they are the main topic for two centuries in the historical record. In archaeology Celtic finds in Norway (numerous and well-catalogues) date from the 9th century, so do Norse finds in Britain. Lastly early Norse place-names are not found on this side of the North Sea. Yet for some reason it has been the habit of Norse scholars to try to argue an earlier settlement. The main arguments for earlier settlements may be stated here.

The Orkneyinga Saga tells how Harald Harfagri extracted a fine of sixty marks of gold from the Orkney early, Torf Einar, for killing the king's son, Halfdan Haaleg. The Earl, we are told, paid the whole on condition that the Orkneymen surrendered their udal rights to him.

The important thing is the use of the word "udal". Bugge and A.W. Johnson argued as follows – This event took place about 895. It took five generations of continuous possession to make land udal. Five generations would take us back to 730 and we can allow another two generations for settlement, which brings us to 664 if we allow 33 years to a generation.

The weakness of the argument is that the only two law codes which could have operated in the islands, the Gulathing and Frostathing, were not codified until two or three centuries after 895, the Gulathing after 1066. The Gula law specified five generations, the Frostathing four. There is no earlier indication as to what constituted udal possession, and no mention of land conquered, as the islands certainly were. Every date based on Harfagri's reign may be a generation too early. And the sagas were not written, at any rate, until the 13th century.

The massacre of St. Donnan in Eigg in 618 and attacks on Tory Islands and Donegal, suggested by some enthusiasts as Norse, agree in neither time nor place.

Shetelig stresses the resemblances of English and Norwegian brooches and animal ornamentation as early as the 6th century. But the ships crossing the North Sea at this time were those of the Angles. He also tries to build a case on the fact that the Scandinavian countries used quartzite and steel instead of flint and steel until the 7th century, and that this was also the use in the islands of Scotland and north-west Ireland. There are two answers. The Norse strike-a-lights were shaped; and islands ones never. Quartzite in these places replaced the flint they did not possess.

Jakobsen's attempts to prove early settlement by the fact that the pre-viking words vin and heim are used in place-names is now largely given up by the Norse themselves. Shetelig's conclusion in 1940 is "It can hardly be contended that the place-names afford evidence of a settlement in the isles appreciably earlier than the year 800."

Clouston has several ingenious arguments in his "History of Orkney." Four large bae farma in Stronsay were broken up. As they are not mentioned in the sagas, they must have been broken up by saga times.

This division of patriarchal farms is a gisn of early settlement. So runs the argument. The answer is that the sagas were written in Iceland; one told of the doings of the Orkney earls, not the place-names of Stronsay. The use of Skaill in Orkney to signify a hall of timber, differing from its use in Norway and Iceland, was probably from the vanity of those who could afford timber halls in a treeless land, and is not a sign of early settlement. The absence of names in "sta" in the smaller isles of Orkney, names popular in Iceland, merely infers settlement by people of lower rank, as does the absence of personal names. Clouston's history has indeed to be read very critically.

What archaeology tells us is this. Out of some 18 Norse finds in Shetland all those datable are 9th or 10th century, or in two cases the Middle Ages. This excludes Jarlshof, which backs it to the latter. Out of 50 Orkney finds, a spearhead, found in a grave at Skaill, is eighth century. We can infer that its owner was buried with an old weapon. Comparative number of finds for other Norse settlements are 12 for the Western Isles, 13 for Caithness and Sutherland, 16 for the Isle of Man, and about 40 to 50 for some nine or ten Irish counties. Dublin, long and viking centre, dwarfs everything with about 150 weapons and as many ornaments and utensils. Out of this mass one sword and shield boss in Arran has been shakily dated to either Anglo-Saxon or 8th century Norse.

Out of the 500 discoveries in Norway, all which can be dated are in 9th or 10th century graves. Personal ornaments and drinking horns belong chiefly to the 9th and swords and balance scales to the 10th. Trade follows the flag. Rogaland and Sogn have a third of the finds between them. In the viking period Norway was still not united, and people from different parts, settling in a small area like Shetland, may have been mutually hostile.

From archaeological finds we can say that in the 9th century there were Norse in Orkney and Westray, Sanday. Rousay and Sandwick, and in Shetland in Sumburgh and Unst. These are positive facts. In arguing from numbers of finds, as the archaeologist has to do, the weakness is that new finds may upset our results. In figures Rogaland has 83, Sogn 70, the Trondelags 61, Vestforld 48, Hordaland 31, Möre 27. The men of Rogaland and Vestfold are likely to have taken the direct route to the Orkneys. For all the others the natural route is that to Shetland, and from

Sogn northwards the first landfall is the North Isles of Shetland. This applied as long as Ireland was the goal. In 872, with the settlement of Iceland, the double stream which earlier converged on Orkney changed to a double stream from Norway and the Hebrides concentrating on Shetland.

For the first two or three years the raids on Ireland came by way of the English Channel. But in 795 Iona was plundered, and in 798 Ulster and the Hebrides were attacked. It would seem that between these years the northern route had been taken, perhaps from the west. Not until 834 do we have any farther attacks on England, for about the year 800 Charlemagne organised the defences between the Elbe and Scheldt and kept the Danes on the defensive. Thus all attacks between these dates came by the northern route. There were sporadic attacks in 802 and 806 on Iona, and along the west coast of Ireland in the three years 811-813. Apart from two visits to the Loire and La Rochelle, there were not more attacks recorded until 820. From 820 no harbour or river was free from the pirate fleets, which came in ever-greater numbers. "The ocean poured torrents of foreigners over Eire." The attacks were yearly. Little permanent groups of invaders were established; in Meath in 826, Arklow 835, Lough Neagh 839, Dublin became a centre of operations from 836. About 847 a Continental annalist reports, "The Scots, after being attacked by Northmen for very many years, were rendered tributary; and the Northmen took possession, without resistance, of the islands that lie all round, and dwelt there." In other words, the Hebrides were then settled.

The pause after the full-scale raids of 812 and 814 bears a striking resemblance to the comparative peace which descended on Ireland at the time of the settlement of Iceland. The raids of 812 have an isolated and piratical appearance. It is therefore very probably that the time from 814 to 820 may have been employed in making settlements in the isles, on the plan employed in Ireland; small communities of Norse living in armed neutrality among people of a foreign race and language. Possibly the northern isles in both groups were first affected. In the nature of things there would have been intermarriage, land purchase of some sort, probably also violent dispossession and migration of the earlier inhabitants. The Norwegian custom of strand-hogg (killing cattle to provision ships) must have hit the islanders hard. But there was no wholesale rooting out yet.

Lewis place-names were once entirely Norse, and are still so in the proportion of 4 to 1, while Skye has 3 to 2 and Islay 1 Norse name to 4 Gaelic. The Isle of Man, long under Norse rule, has 1 Norse name to 8 Celtic. Here out of 41 names on Manx rune grave crosses 26, and 2 surnames, are Norse and 15 Celtic. A father with a Norse name has a son with a Celtic one, and a Celt orders a cross from a Norse rune carver. In other words, there was a mixture of races.

Such particular accounts as bear on the invasion of Shetland may now be given in a concise way. First Dicuil, an Irish Monk, living about 825.

"This is now the thirtieth year from the time when I was informed by priests who had remained in that island from Kalends of February to the Kalends of August, that not only in the summer solstice, but in the days on both sides of it the sun setting in the evening hour hides itself as it were behind a little knoll." This they thought to be Thule (Iceland) and a day's sail to the north would bring them into the frozen sea. "There are in the northern ocean of Britain many other islands which can be reached in two days' and two nights' straight sailing with a steady wind blowing favourably from the northern islands of Britain. A religious priest related to me that he had entered one of them in two summer days and one intervening night, sailing in a boat with two thwarts. Some of these islands are small; nearly all alike are separated by narrow channels, and in them for nearly a hundred years hermits have dwelt, sailing from our Scotia (Ireland). But just as from the beginning of the world they were ever uninhabited, so now because of those robbers the Northmen they are empty of hermits, though full of innumerable sheep and very many kinds of sea birds." The route to the Faroes via Orkney and Shetland was thus blocked in 825.

Now an entirely confused Irish fragment by one Duald Mac Firbis.

"Not long before this" (i.e. the taking of York in 867 by the Danes) "there was all manner of war and strife in Lochlann" (Scandinavian) "and that war in Lochlann arose out of this, that two young sons of Halfdan, king of Lochlann, had expelled the eldest son, Ronald, Halfdan's son, for fear he should take the kingdom of Lochlann after their father. And Ronald came with his three sons to the Orkney Islands. Then Ronald remained there with his youngest son, but the older sons came to the islands of Britain with a great host" ... "They thought that their father would go to Scandinavia at once after they departed."

The account goes on to tell how they plundered in Spain and Morocco, and how before a battle one of the brothers told the other that it had been revealed to him in a dream that their father was along now, in a land which did not belong to him, because one of the sons left with him had been slain, "and his other son has been killed in a battle; and the father himself scarcely escapes out of that battle."

The expedition of the account, led by Hastein and Björn, plundered from Spain to north-western Italy between 859 and 862.

The **Historia Norwegiae** was written in the last quarter of the 12th century, and is a Norwegian account, in Latin.

"Certain islands lie before the Gulathing district, and are named Sulend Isles by the inhabitants; from them is named the Solundic Sea, which flows between Norway and Ireland. In it are the Orchades Islands, more than thirty in number, named after an earl, Orchanus. These, occupied by different inhabitants are now divided into two dominions, the southern islands (i.e. Hebrides) are elevated to kinglets, while the northern are adorned by the protection of earls; and both pay large tribute to the kings of Norway.

"Of the Orchades Islands – these islands were at first inhabited by the Peti and Papea. Of these the one race, the Peti, little exceeded pigmies in stature; they did marvels in the morning and the evening in building towns, but at mid-day they entirely lost all their strength, and lurked, through fear, in little underground houses.

"But at that time they were not called Orchades, but Pictland; whence still the Pictland Sea is named by the inhabitants, because it divides the islands from Scotland.

"And the Papae have been named from their white robes, which they wore like priests; whence priests are all called "papae" in the Teutonic tongue. An island is still called after them, Papey. But as is observed from their habit and the writings of their books abandoned there, they were Africans, adhering to Judaism.

"In the days of Harold Fairhair, king of Norway, certain pirates, of the family of the most vigorous prince Ronald, set out with a great fleet and crossed the Solundic sea, and stripped these races of their ancient settlements, destroyed them utterly, and subdued the islands to themselves. And being there provided with safe winter seats, they went in summer working tyranny upon the English and the Scots, sometimes also upon the Irish, so that they took under their rule from England, Northumbria; and from Scotland, Caithness; from Ireland, Dublin and other seaports."

It is interesting that the last inhabitants of Jarlshof did live in an underground house, when the wheelhouses were in ruin, and that the tradition of Pictish dwarfs living underground was known to old people in my boyhood. This, the only Norwegian account, for the sagas were Icelandic, would account in a wholesale way for the disappearance of place-names.

To clarify the saga accounts we must mention Harald Harfagri. He is assumed to have been born about 854 and to have died at the age of eighty. He was ten when he came to the throne, and according to the sagas, twenty when he overcame the combined fleets of his enemies at Hafrsfjord. Many Norwegian authorities, however, place the union of Norway after Hafrsfjord in 900 or 910. There are good reasons for doubting the dates implied in the sagas, the excessive length (some seventy years) of Harfagri's reign, saga mistakes in the implied dating of foreign events, and the probability that Hafrsfjord and colonisation of Iceland are put at the same time through the wrong inference that the latter was the result of the former. With this proviso, here are some saga accounts - **Saga of Harald Harfagri** (Heimskringla) (written in Iceland 1220-1237).

"Rognvald, Earl of Möre, a son of Eystein Glumre, had the summer before become one of Harald's men; and the king set him as chief over these two districts. North Möre and Raumsdal; strengthened him both with fighting men and farmers, and gave him the help of ships to defend the coast against enemies. He was called Rognvald the Mighty, or the Wise, and people say both names suited well.

"In the discontent that King Harald seized on the lands of Norway, the out-countries of Iceland and the Faroe Isles were discovered and peopled. The Northmen had also a great going to Shetland, and many men left Norway as outlaws flying the country on account of King Harald and went viking cruises into the west sea. In winter they were in the Orkneys and Hebrides; but plundered in summer in Norway, and did great damage.

"King Harald heard that the Vikings, who were in the west sea in winter, plundered far and wide in the middle part of Norway; and therefore every summer he made an expedition to search the isles and outskerries on the coast. Wherever the Vikings heard of him they all took to flight, and most of them out into the open ocean. At last the king grew weary of this work, and therefore one summer he sailed with his fleet right out into the West Sea. First he came to Shetland, and he slew all the Vikings who could not save themselves by flight." He proceeded to Orkney, the Hebrides, plundered in Scotland, and found the Isle of Man abandoned.

"In this war fell Ivar, son of Rognvald, Earl of Möre, and King Harald gave Rognvald, as a compensation for the loss, the Orkney and Shetland Isles, when he sailed form the west, but Rognvald immediately gave these countries to his brother Sigurd, who remained behind in them, and King Harald, before sailing eastward, gave Sigurd the earldom of them."

The Saga of St. Olaf (earliest part of Heimskringla) "It is said that in the days of Harald the Fairhaired, King of Norway, the Orkneys were peopled, but before that they were a viking lair. Sigurd was the name of the first Earl of Orkney, he was the son of Eystein Glumra, and brother of Rognvald, Earl of Möre."

Egil's Saga (12 century). "But from this enslavement (to Harfagri) fled many away out of the land, and then began to be settled many waste parts both far and wide, both east in Jamtaland and Helsingland, and in the west countries; the Hebrides, Dublin county in Ireland, Normandy in France, Caithness in Scotland, the Orkneys and Shetland, the Faroes. And in that time was found Iceland."

Svarfdoela Saga. "Then many noble men in Norway had fled from their udal lands, and some went west beyond the sea to Shetland and Orkney, and settled there; and many went to Iceland, and that began now to be very fully inhabited."

Olaf Tryggvason's Saga. (13th century). "One summer Harald Harfagri went to the west across the sea to punish the Vikings, as he was weary of their devastations. They plundered in Norway during the summer and spent the winters in Shetland and Orkneys. Harald subdued Shetland, the Orkneys and the Hebrides. He went west as far as the Isle of Man, and destroyed all the dwellings in Man. He fought many battles there, and extended his dominium so far to the west that none of the kings of Norway since his time has had wider dominions. In one of these battles Ivar, the son of Earl Rognvald, fell. So when King Harald sailed from the west he gave Shetland and the Orkneys to Earl Rognvald as a compensation for his son, but Earl Rognvald gave the islands to his brother Sigurd, who was King Harald's forecastleman; and the king gave him the title of earl before he left the west. Sigurd remained out in the west."

The Danish-Icelandic historian Torfaeus. "Orkney was of old a nest of pirates that aspired to the dominion of the northern seas, until they were at last extirpated by Harold the Fair, king of Norway, who gifted Orkney and Shetland to one of his nobles, named Ronald. This Ronald gave these islands to his **son** Sigurd, who was created an earl by King Harold and who was the first who bore the title Earl of Orkney."

Bishop Thomas Tulloch of Orkney (1446). "We find that in the time of Harald Fairhair, first king of Norway, who throughout his reign possessed this province of insular country, Orkney was inhabited and cultivated by two tribes, namely the Peti and the Pape, which two classes of people were utterly overthrown and eradicated by Norwegians of the clan or tribe of the most valiant prince Rognvald, who fell upon these tribes, the Peti and the Pape, so that no remnant of their posterity hath been left. It is true, however, that this country was not then called Orcadia, but the land of the Pets, as is clearly confirmed, with the additional attestation of a chronicle still extant, by the sea separating Scotland and Orkney, which even to this day is dominated by the Petland Sea. This king, Harald the Fairhaired, arrived with his fleet first in Shetland and subsequently in Orkney, and conferred Orkney and Shetland on the aforesaid prince, Rognvald the Mighty, but whose clan, as was premised, the two tribes aforenamed had been overthrown and uprooted. The most valiant prince Rognvald gifted the same Earldom freely and absolutely to a certain brother of his, Siward by name."

The saga accounts are consistent enough, but they are mostly taken one from another, and they are three or four centuries after the events they narrate. Bishop Tulloch is relying on the Historia Norwegiae. The difficulty in accepting the saga accounts is the matter of dating. Thus a certain Thorgils, given as Harfagri's son in this saga, and "the first of the Northmen who took Dublin" was drowned by the Irish in 845, before Harfagri was born, and Ketil Flatneb, said to be sent by Harfagri to subdue the Vikings in the Hebrides, was certainly there before Harfagri's birth. Harfagri is variously said to have made one and two expeditions to the west, but it is unlikely that he could have don so until 890 to 900, while Sigurd was in Orkney in 872 (he is named with the Pope, the Emperor, the Emperor of Constantinople, and the kings of Norway, Sweden, Denmark, England and Dublin in fixing the time of the settlement of Iceland). The sagas, if fact, are repeating a Norwegian propaganda claim to the overlordship of Orkney. There is no evidence at all barring the one account repeated in Harfagri's and Olaf Tryggvason's saga, that he granted the earldom to Rognvald, who transferred it to Sigurd. Orkney was brought first under Norwegian control by Magnus Barefoot about 1100. The sagas lump all Norse settlements into Harfagri's reign, which they obviously were not.

Sigurd the Mighty warred in the north of Scotland until he died of blood poisoning from the tooth of his enemy, whose head he had hung at his saddle bow. His companion in the invasion, Thorstein the Red, fell in battle. This may have happened in 875. Sigurd's son Guttorm ruled for a winter, and died without children. Here is a composite account from the sagas of his successor.

"When Rognval, Earl of Möre, heard of the death of Sigurd his brother and his son, and also that Vikings sat in those lands, both in Shetland and in the Orkney's, he sent his son Hallad west, who took the name of earl to begin with. He had many fighting men with him. When he arrived in the Orkneys he settled there in the autumn and in winter, and in the spring times Vikings sailed about the islands and the coast of Caithness, killing men, plundering the headlands, and killing cattle on the shore. But when the farmers complained of their wrongs before Hallad, it seemed to him in the isles (and) grew tired of his high rank. He gave up his earldom, took the rank of udaller, and afterwards returned east to Norway. And men thought his expedition a great joke. When Earl Rognvald heard of this he was ill-pleased with Hallad, and said his sons were very unlike their ancestors."

The story of Hallad's brother Torf Einar, who succeeded him as earl, and ruled the northern islands and the north mainland of Scotland, bringing order out of chaos, is too long to tell. In his lifetime his brother Rollo was ruling in Normandy, Iceland was rapidly filling up with settlers, and the colonisation of the islands was complete.

Apart from those given, there are hardly any early references to Shetland in the saga. "Floki Vilgerdson was the name of a great viking. He set out from Rogaland to search for Iceland ... He sailed first to Shetland and lay in Floki's Bay; there his daughter Geirhild was lost in Geirhild's water." Floki was the first to go to Iceland on set purpose. The story is associated with Girsta – Geirhild's farm, and she is traditionally said to have fallen through the ice in the loch there.

According to the Fljotsdoela Saga, Thorvald, a younger brother of Ketil Thrym, a settler in Iceland, came to Shetland, where he married Droplaug, daughter of an earl called Bjorgolf, an old man who then ruled over Shetland. The Droplaugarsona Saga gives another account of Droplaug's parentage, so we do not know if Bjorgolf is historical or mythical.

Mousa broch was for the first time in written record when Bjorn Brynjulfson and Thora Lace-Hand spent part of their elopement period there.

There is a tradition in the North Isles that Harfagri first made land at Finyie in Fetlar and then made his way from there to Haroldswick, but as he is said to be buried there in a cairn called Harald's Grave, we have all the makings of a late folk tale. There seems to be a more ancient tradition that the first boat of Norse settlers came to Finyie, and went round to and settled in now-deserted Grütin.

the picture of the Norse occupation presented as a whole is this. Previously the islands were thinly peopled, by Picts, among whom were settlements of Celtic clergy, the Peti and Papae of the Norse account. From archaeological evidence there were Norse settlers in the first half of the 9th century in the North Isles of both Shetland and Orkney and at Sumburgh. From the historical evidence it seems that the Picts were first disturbed a year or two previous to 800, and that there was limited and localised settlements by about 820. Life in the islands must have been from that time a continuous struggle. The custom of strand-hogg, landing and slaying animals to provision the ships, was permissible in Norway, and as the raiding ships came in late spring and returned in autumn, the islanders must have suffered doubly. If the inhabitants possessed ships there was no doubt a considerable emigration to Scotland. Probably, when slaves were a commodity for which there was a ready market in

Ireland and Norway, there was little security in person as well as in property. Finally, about 860, viking fleets from Möre "stripped these races of their ancient settlements, destroyed them utterly, and subdued the islands to themselves." Sigurd carried the conquest into Caithness and Sutherland about 870, and there the Norse were fought to a standstill. Lastly, in the time of the Icelandic migration, Shetland was a rendezvous of people, of whom the wealthier and more adventurous sought the greater opportunities of Iceland, while the more ordinary folk contented themselves with purchasing or otherwise obtaining a place among the abandoned homesteads of the Picts.

CHAPTER 4 _____

The Evidence of Place Names

WHAT is described as a farm below may be land belonging to a person, or to a dozen owners. In Shetland it is called a "toon", which is in Norse written "tun".

Names vary according to time. A purely English name like Fairview would not have been given a century ago, nor would Roadside, for there were no roads to speak of. On the other hand, Maryfield or Knowe or Hillhead or Linthouse belong to the Scots fashion, and are older. Pund came in at the time of the very first Scots settlers, and Vatzhool dates itself, for "vatns" changed to "vatz" about the 13th century.

If we can prove that names survive in bulk which were in use in Norway before 800, then both the historical and archaeological records need to be reconsidered. If we can prove that there is a difference with Faroe and Iceland which were settled mostly after 872, we may have a case for an earlier settlement of Shetland. Like considerations apply to the other Scots settlements.

Names may differ in space as well as time. The settlers came from Norway, and Norway is an extensive country. Place-names common in some districts were hardly used at all in another. If therefore we find certain place-names in bulk in a district in Norway and again in a Norwegian colony, we may expect the original settlers to have come from there. There, of course, could be later comers, just as there have been Scots, who arrived after naming had taken place.

There is also the social difference. The names Cottage, Villa, House, give us pictures of different buildings. In Norse days these differences of rank were of considerably greater account than at any time since, and the nature of the farm can often be guessed from the name.

It will perhaps be easiest to dispose of the names which Jakobsen, and others following him, have suggested as proof of early settlement. The first, "heimr", means dwelling, like the English ham, not home as we understand it. (Note – Shetland ham means harbour, akin to the English word haven). There are about 1,100 old heim names in Norway, and of these many scores cannot be interpreted from Old Norse. They are assumed to date from 400 to 600 A.D. but 25 to 30 have been found in Iceland. Jakobsen found 10 names in Shetland which might be heim names. Of these the only two certainties are Digeren and Sullom, both of which occur more than once in Norway. In fact, Sullom (sun farm) occurs over 70 times. Here we simply have a settler naming his new farm after his old. No case but a negative can therefore be built up from heim names.

Vin, meaning pasture, is assumed to belong to the second or third century of our era, and neither occurs in Iceland nor Faroe. The 1,100 farms in Norway are mostly disguised, ending in –e, -en, or –in, like Vigre, Moen, Sendin. Jakobsen found a number of vin names in Shetland, and for a time this was the chief argument for early settlement. But the Shetland names are radically different. They begin with vin or win, and they are never used of farms. There are no names of the Norwegian type either in Shetland or in Orkney.

The position of Celtic names may be stated thus. The Norse borrowed from the Celts new ways of doing things, together with the technical words involved; the Celts borrowed words in general, and more of them. In Iceland and Faroe there are undoubted place-names incorporating Celtic personal names, but part of the immigration to Iceland was from the Hebrides and Ireland. Njal, the hero of the greatest saga, is simply the Celtic Neil.

Jakobsen, however, proposed to find some 30 general Welsh and Gaelic place-names. In every case where I have been able to apply a test the meaning suggested is unsuitable, and the word is readily explained from Norse. The portion on Celtic place-names does not bear the stamp of authority of Jakobsen's actual field-work, and cannot at all be used as evidence of a Celtic population which intermingled with the Norse.

Are there any place-names at all in Shetland which are older than Norse? It is not very easy to say. All the main names, parishes, most islands, hills, voes, capes, lakes, etc., are undoubtedly Norse. There is a certain number of names so changed that any attempt at their meaning can only be a guess. But if a guess is to be made it is safe to stick to Norse, for while a Norse name may have taken on an unrecognisable garb with the passing of centuries, it is fantastic to derive meanings from sources so far apart as Welsh and Gaelic. If any altered original names survive, perhaps Shetland itself, Yell, Unst, Fetlar, may be four, for these, of the major names, are difficult, but what language they can be explained from is another matter.

What this implies it is difficult to say. But although we have aboriginal names in Australia, and pre-Columban words in the West Indies, it would be probably be unsafe to say that the eradication of an incompatible language over a long period infers the complete disappearance of the race that spoke it.

The oldest types of names used in Shetland are descriptive words without any article or other embellishment, words like Sand or Mail (sand), Skaw (a cape), Week Soond, Strand, Voe, Ham (harbour), Hamar (rock outcrop), Clett, Daal, Hool (small hill), Break (slope), Lee (slope), etc. The great number of these "monosyllabic" names are original, but often another word is added for distinguishing purposes, as Sandwick, Westerwick.

It is possible to separate some names historically. There are many papers going back to the 16th century and one or two to the 13th. But often a name late as a farm name may be early as a place name.

The commonest endings for farm names in order of frequency are gert, setter, hoose, toon, field (partly English, partly the Old Norse fjall), ness, land, pund (Scots), daal, break, broch, lee, week, voe, sta, bister, and quoy.

Of these perhaps the most interesting are three of the earliest; sta, bister and setter names. Whereas there are no farm names ending in "vin" in Shetland, and possibly only two or three in heim compared with 1,100 of each in Norway; there are 163 setters in Shetland compared with 1,100 in Norway, and 47 bisters to 97 in Norway. Setr, however, is neither found in Iceland nor Faroe, although bister names occur in Iceland in the form "bol". Sta is a short form of stathir, a higher class of farm, which occurs 3000 times in Norway, is by far the commonest ending in Iceland, where it occurs 1165 times, and 47 times in Shetland. All these names appear to have been used originally, but the setter names had the longest life, and in some cases became confused with another word "saetr", a shieling or place where cattle grazed in summer. It is the smallest of the three types of farms, and consists of land generally lying between the best settlements, which may have been expected to be chosen latest. The bister type of farm is bigger, and often occurs two or three together, or is a place which is subdivided. Bolstathr (bister) was very common in the Scots colonies, as it occurs 50 times in Orkney and 157 times in the Norse parts of Scotland, a far greater number than in Norway itself. Both bister and setter names are found most commonly in Norway in Sogn and Möre, which agrees well enough with the saga evidence. Stathir (sta) farms are bigger still, and usually have as the first part the personal name of their owner. In Norway they occur in the inland district from Oslo to Trondhjem, and Shetland has more of them than either Orkney or the other Norse settlements in Scotland.

The absence of setr in Faroe is probably because it was settled as a half-way house to Iceland. The settlers in Iceland were men of rank, whose land-takings were much larger than what was implied by setr.

The sta names are often second generation names in Iceland, bearing not the names of the original settlers but of their sons and grandsons. They are particularly common in the south-west of Norway where the present-day speech shows affinities with the Shetland dialect. They may be the farms of latecomers, who arrived in Shetland when the Icelandic migration was in full swing.

About 77 farm names in Shetland end in land, as compared with 2350 in Norway and 84 in Iceland. This ending is common in Shetland, however, for field names, but usally in the form of "lands". More than half the land names are in West Agder and Rogaland in Norway, from which the Shetland dialect is supposedly derived. Both in Norway and Iceland the land farms were in the nature of outsets, and continued to be given from pre-Viking to Christian times. In Shetland the land farms are generally on high, rather out-of-the-way ground, but they are larger than setter farms on the average.

Other names which have an early stamp end in wick and voe, and it is natural that the vicinity of these should be settled earlier than the nesses. Broch (Old Norse borg) seems early in every case, and no doubt the settlers found ready-made shelters in the ruins of these.

Names which require to be hand-picked are the very numerous ones in gert, gord, gerdie, gerdin, etc. They represent two Old Norse words, garthr and gerthi, and cover a long period. In some parts of Shetland they are absent as farm names, but they are found both in Orkney and the Hebrides.

Quoy (Old Norse "kvi") and pund were cattle enclosures which became farms. The latter does not occur in Norway but is a Scots word adopted in Norse times. Hoose (hus) marks the first udal subdivision, but is also used at the present day. The usual formula in a "toon" was Northus, Esthus, Wasthus, Soothus, Uphus, Mews (i.e. Mid house), Nisthus (nethermost house) and so on. Some of these names became farm names.

A considerable collection of Norse place-names has now been made, and it is hoped to publish some of the results soon. In their spoken form they are close to the Old Norse as most Norwegian names, but there is nothing in them to indicate that Shetland was settled earlier than the other Norse islands of Scotland. In particular, the old pre-viking words for farm, heim, and vin, cannot be used as evidence. Heim occurs in Sullom, which is found over seventy times in Norway, and Digeren or Dikkeren, which is found twice in Shetland, and a great many times in Norway. These names may be put in awkward English as Sunny farm and Substantial farm. Sodom in Whalsay is not Sudheim, but a ham or harbour name. It is a late outset names from Hamister, the harbour setter, which lies on the north side of the same valley.

The use of vin in Shetland is quite different from Norway. In Norwegian place-names it occurs at the end of a word, usually in the form of –in or –e. In Shetland it is at the beginning and is never a farm name. The only exceptions are Levenwick and Levaneep, where the first part is probably leik-vin, a compound word meaning a place where sports, such as horse-racing and athletic contests of various kinds were held.

Besides the names mentioned the following words seem to have been favourites with the early settlers: öy (island), skagi (cape), sund (sound), sandr (sand), fjörthr (now reduced to firt), gnupr (our word noup, a headland), öyrr (our word air, a beach), eith (an isthmus), melr (sand), topt (Shetland taft, a place with older foundations), völlr (a field), brekka (a slope or foothill), hlith (our word lee, an unbroken slope), hamarr (a

47

rock outcrop), fjall or fell which easily becomes "field"; a hill). Holl (Shetland holl, a small hill, equivalent to the Scots word knowe and dair (Shetland daal, a valley) are so numerous that they are found as farm names everywhere. Among human activities occur tun (a group of crofts), kirk (which is not likely to be earlier than the 11th century), haugr, a mound, and skali, a shed or outhouse; possibly in the islands a building made of timber. Generally speaking, our ancestors were matter-of-fact people, who named their surroundings plainly from what they saw, but in doing so they used nearly all the words which one can find as place-names in Norway or elsewhere in the Norse colonies. The only exceptions are words concerned with timber-working, and words which were in use in Norway before the isles were settled and after close connection with them were lost. Otherwise, one might take a stretch of coast in Norway and in Shetland, and by changing a few letters get practically the same result. Here, for Shetlanders, are a few common adjectives which occur again and again. Gamla (old), nee (new), swarta (black), wheeda (white), rö (red), gul (yellow), gruna (green), blo (blue), gro (grey), jupi (deep), bretta (steep), flada (flat), mö and mio (narrow), brae (broad), lunga (long), bolli (round). There are many others. It is a great pity that in our new housing we are adopting namby-pamby English names, which are quite unsuitable, and at the same time letting the good old Norse names disappear as croft after croft becomes a sheeprun. But such is the price of activity, for it would be hardly suitable to call it the price of progress.

The actual written forms of croft names are common after 1500, and we can follow them practically continuously from the last half of that century. A few earlier written forms go back to the 13th century. But there is little doubt that the bulk of our place-names are as old as they seem, and are to be interpreted in plain, matter-of-fact Old Norse. Of anything older there is no evidence, except for a hint in the name Shetland itself, and perhaps a main name or two like the word Unst, which may be glosses of older words. Anyone who searches for Celtic roots is wasting his time.

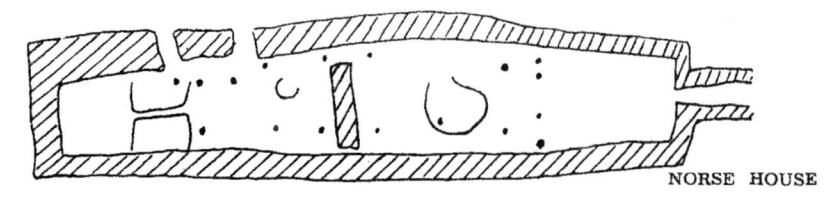

NORSE HOUSE

CHAPTER 5

Norse and Christian Remains

IT might be thought that Norse remains, starting about 800 A.D. would be more common than those of earlier ages. This, however, is not so, from a simple reason. To begin with, our ancestors were no builders in stone. A low, broad wall, four or five feet high and three to five thick, consisting of an outer and inner skin of stone, with the centre filled with turf and earth, was the acme of their skill in house-building. Sometimes there were alternate courses of turf and earth. There was no attempt to lay stones through to bind the outer and inner walls, nor were the stones above laid so as to cover the joints between those below and bind them together. There was no proper building in courses or layers, and no quarrying to find suitable stones. The result was a wall full of vertical cracks and bulges, with the outer and inner skins ready to part company, only upheld by its extreme width in relation to height.

This type of building continued in a modified form in country districts until the present century, when concrete largely replaced stone. The wall had certainly become narrower (2 ½ to 3 feet) and higher, but the average croft building had no coursing, few binding stones which lay through the wall from inside to outside, and very little attempt to prevent vertical cracks. On the outside, before mortar or concrete came into vogue, it was stopped with moss, on the inside with clay. The centre, instead of mortar, was filled with earth.

None of the old croft houses, now so rapidly being abandoned, are of any great age. Aage Roussell, who investigated Norse houses in Shetland previous to the war, mentions six, but these are merely ordinary houses a century of so old. Briefly, such houses were more or less of Scots type, 30 feet long by 12 broad inside, but perpetuating the Norse love of masonry. Old Norse houses were longer, narrower, lower, and differed in other ways.

They have not survived for two main reasons. First the land has been in continuous occupation and the houses have been pulled down and replaced time and again. Secondly they were badly built, and if any foundations were left on the occasions when a new site was chosen, these were easily removed to be used in outhouses and walls.

Any proper masonry, such as the work on Scalloway and Muness castles (both about 1600), the work on churches (including the now-vanished steepled ones at Papil in Burra, Ireland, and Tingwall), on the little castle in the Loch of Strom, and elsewhere, was done by masons coming from the south. Any foundation with mortar is later than the 12 century, when St. Magnus' Cathedral was begun.

It would be particularly valuable in Shetland to list the sites of all abandoned houses. Very few of them are likely to be early, as in general the places which, being poorer land, were occupied last, have been abandoned first. The division of land into separate crofts has gone on for little more than 150 years. Before that time, and still in the period of Scots influence, which may be said to date from 1550 onwards, the land was held in common, each house having a rig (Scots) or teg (Old Norse teigr, a measured strip of land) in the cultivated parts, and a daal or dil or dild (Old Norse deild, a portion) in the grassland. In some places the instinct for fair play seems to have been so pronounced that these were exchanged from year to year, but usually in the latter times they were held by one owner. Here again it would be invaluable if anyone who remembers what the routine was like before the land in his district was planked (i.e. divided into separate crofts) could describe it before it is too late. In one case I know of there was one field which was heavily manured, set to bere, and laboured in common by six neighbours in addition to their own separate parts, and the occasion of this field's harvesting was a general feast and rejoicing.

This system of land-holding, the result often of udal subdivision of land equally among sons, led to a communal way of life in many parts. The Old Norse bygth easily became the Scots biggin, five or six houses with their byres, barns and so on built in insanitary and close proximity. Farther away were lambhouses, skeos for drying fish and meat, and houses for geese. On the nearest burns were their mills. Outhouses often included sheds for wood-working. At the shore were the nowsts or noosts

(Old Norse naust) for the open boats. Pigs and ponies ran wild in the hills, and the former were in the 16th century regarded as such a nuisance that their owners were fined for possessing them.

Of these adjuncts to a croft few are now to be seen. The word nowst is still used for a beach where a boat is drawn up, but the built naust, a U-shaped place for a boat with built sides perhaps two or three feet high, is hardly to be seen except at the abandoned fishing station of Fethaland. There is only one roofed naust, as far as I know, in the islands, at Collaster in Sandness, which has a wood and turf roof and doors which completely protect the boat from the weather. Only one old Shetland mill, at Troswick, is in working order. It has a wooden roof, but otherwise is the normal style of old Shetland mill. There is, mercifully, no skeo in the whole country, although their foundations may be seen at Garthsness, Quendale and elsewhere. Unroofed fishermen's lodges, where the men rested between spells at the haaf, or deep sea line fishing, may be found at Fethaland and Stenness, and there are many places round the shore where old booths, a few still roofed, can be seen. These were for supplies to the fishermen and reception of their catches. Some were originally for German merchants and have been occupied sites from the 15th century.

All these things were in use till the end of last century, and go back to a respectable antiquity. The old type of mill was certainly in use in the 16th century, when Lord Robert Stewart interfered with the udal mills of Orkney, but it is much older both in Norway and the Norse colonies. Place-names such as Snekkerom and Skuddanaust tell us of a time when the snekkja, a fast type of viking ship, protected the islands, and the skuda, a kind of 10 or 12 oared ship, made voyages to Norway.

There is a certain number of older Norse house sites. Nine are found at Jarlshof. There is said to be one at Mousa; there is at least one practically washed away by the sea at Sandwick in Unst; two others are at Fjel and Bighton in the Westing of Unst, one at least, as well as medieval houses, at the Sands of Bracon in North Yell, and one, overlaid by later building, close to the roadside at Eshaness, Northmaven. Normally late houses face the sea, but older ones are often on a slope with the gable to the sea. The most likely places for really ancient houses to survive is where there is sand in motion, as at Jarlshof itself, Quendale and the other parts of Dunrossness where the estate of Broo and the toons of Lee, Lobel and

Udelsgarth lie buried, in Bracon and Papil in Yell, and in Sandwick in Unst. Normally all traces have been removed by rebuilding.

The Old Norse house was made up of the stofa (chief living room), skali (sleeping room), eldhus (kitchen) and bur (larder). Stove and Skail are still used in place-names. The bur (pronounced boor) may have been detached. The house was very narrow (perhaps 10 or 11 feet inside) and probably five or six times as long. In a large farm there would be a dyngja, or women's room, a bathstofa for steam baths, a skemma, or storehouse for meat, and a smithja or smithy, but these have not been found at Jarlshof, although bathstofa occurs in Shetland place-names. The outbuildings were fjarhus for sheep, fjos for cattle, hesthus of stable, hlatha or barn, and kvi or sheepfold. The latter, really an enclosure, was our kwy, written quoy, and was followed in time by the Scots word pund, which signified a complete rounded wall, or a curved wall cutting off part of the shore, or perhaps a straight wall across a headland.

The house had its door in the side wall, and there might be a stett, or narrow pavement, in front of the side wall, a stiggi (stile or pathway) leading from the house, or a strodi, or narrow lane leading from one end.

Badly-built as the walls were, the roof rested on the inner one, so the whole building was damp. In the stofa, a raised wooden floor called the pallr, about three or four feet wide, ran along each side wall and sometimes along one end, and it was here that the benches, for food and recreation, were placed. At the inner edge of the pallr was a line of upright posts helping to support the roof couples. Along the mid floor there could be several fires, the smoke of which escaped by a hole in the roof. Light was supplied through this and other openings, as well as the open doorway and the artificial light of the fires and kolli, or oil lamp.

In the skali there was a raised turf or wooden flooring called the set, which was divided into sleeping places.

In a kitchen at Jarlshof a box-oven made of stones was found beside the fire. Stones, heated in the fire, were put into the oven, which measured 2 ½ feet by 1 foot 9 inches. Above the stones grass was placed, and on this the food. This was covered with more grass, then more heated stones, then earth or turf. The Jarlshof people seem to have been great fishermen, as numerous bones of ling, cod, saithe and lythe were found.

The spindle and whorl was still used for spinning. Two important pieces of furniture were the hand-mill, or rotary quern, and the loom. Both the hand-mill and the even older knockin-steen or mortar, with its mell or hammer, were used for grinding until last century. In Shetland the taxes were paid in fish oil, butter and wadmel, a course tweed made on the loom, which was so common that we are quite uncertain which of the numerous perforated stones were sinkers and which were loom-weights. A rope network in the rafters called a terry (Old Norse taugreip) in use up to 70 years ago, held fishing gear and various odds and ends.

These long, narrow houses seem to have been in use for four or five centuries. Later houses were of shorter and wider pattern. There are foundations at the Sands of Quendale and at Bracon in Yell. Two large rectangular buildings are in unusual places, which have been fortified, one at Lambhoga Head, not far south of Voe, Boddam, and another on the Hold of Califf in Dales Voe. In the islands of West Linga (Whalsay) there is a complete steading abandoned in the 18th century. A number of houses at Kirkholm, Selie Voe, reputedly built by Armada survivors, are of the dimensions of Old Norse houses. All these sites need to be examined. However, the difference between Norse and everything before it, with the very doubtful exception of a kirk or two, is in more or less straight walling with corners which meet at right angles. All older building is oval or circular in nature.

Most of the house ruins that can be seen elsewhere are 19th century, when Shetland's population was greatest, and these are often outsets. Mousa had 11 families in 1770, but in 1600 it was a grazing isle, as it is now. The houses of the larger udal families have disappeared, replaced by the 18th and 19th century haas of their Scots successors, which now stand empty everywhere, at Tangwick, Swarister, Old Haa at Symbister, Garderhouse and so on. Only five houses are mentioned in the Inventory of Shetland monuments, all of them late 17th or early 18th century; Busta, Vaila, Brough in Burravoe, Jarlshof, and 99 Commercial Street, the oldest building in Lerwick. Underneath a heap of bent and sand on the Links of Quendale, in conditions where the moving sand prevents excavation, lies the Old Haa of Broo, where in 1550 resided Olla Sinclair, the last foud or Governor of Shetland. In all the original "toons" there are sites which are age old, but because man when he rebuilds must pull down, the chances of a house surviving are small indeed. The pre-Norse sites remained mostly because they were outside the areas of Norse settlement.

The numerous churches and chapels, now mostly mere sites, are mainly Norse. Here again a roofless ruin may be quite modern. Papil in Burra is an ancient pre-Norse site; the ruin at present standing is the third on the same place and dates from 1814. Baliasta in Unst was one of the foremost Norse churches, but the present ruin was built in 1746. The Norse, when they started building churches in the 12th century, accepted Christianity with the same enthusiasm with which they had at one time indulged in piracy. Every scattald had its church or chapel, which might be in the care of the chief udaller, and hence places like Fetlar and Unst, which had a very dense population in early Norse times, were blessed with great numbers of chapels, ten or more in the case of Fetlar and over twenty in Unst. Some of these were quite humble buildings, whose sites are all that is known, but others were more important.

In dating early sites we cannot go by architectural features, for little but foundations is left, and these may not be original. But we have Ogam (Irish) writing, carved stones of Irish type and names to go by. So we can assume that Papil, Burra, with its tradition of "nine priests" was in being in the 8th century or earlier, and was still flourishing in the 11th, when someone "raised a stone" in memory of a friend, and carved the words in Norse runes. At St. Ninian's Isle, Mail in Cunningsburgh, and Culliesbrough in Bressay we have oghams, and we are quite safe in saying these are at least 9th century. Mail again has Norse runes, which argues that it, too, survived the Norse heathen period. South Whiteness had a 10th century Irish cross, and Sandness had a 9th century Pictish symbol of the opposing Pictish church, the only one found in Shetland except on a disc at Jarlshof. Lastly we have the name Papa given by the Norse to Irish priests, in Papa Stour, Papa Little, and Papa of Scalloway; and Papil (priest's farm) in Unst, Yell, and Fetlar as well as Burra.

This, of course, is not to say that excavations like those that have taken place recently at St. Ninian's Isle have any prehistoric significance. This chapel according to Brand, was in use in 1701, and it was only about forty years later that the isle was abandoned for lack of fuel, and the chapel torn down by John Bruce Stewart of Symbister, who had married the heiress of

Bigton. But somewhere on the island, if they could only be found, are probably more ogam inscriptions of the old Irish church.

Obviously there must be many ancient sites which can show neither carved stones nor ogam writing. But Brecon in Eshaness has furnished another rune-stone in addition to the spurious one which still lies in the churchyard, and at Framgord in Unst there are hog-backed tombstones, not unlike an upturned boat, which in England can be 9th century. Slabs carved with crosses have been found at Papil, Framgord and St. Ninian's Isle, and very rude tombstones cut in the shape of a cross are found at Uyea, Lund and Norwick in Unst, Reafirth in Yell and North Roe. These date from Catholic times, that is, before 1560.

Ordinary finds from early Norse times can be quickly enumerated. In Unst last century much as dug up and left unrecorded. At Houlland, near the Loch of Cliff, four "cleeber" bowls were found. At Sandwick there must be abundant relics and three combs have been found. At Clibberswick a woman's grave was found in a farmyard, with two oval bronze brooches, a trefoil bronze brooch, two glass beads and a silver armlet. Also from Unst came an oval brooch with 9th century ornament and a bronze case for holding a balance. Gold finger rings are recorded from Marrister, Whalsay, and Lunnasting, a gold wire bracelet from Oxna, a penannular 10th century brooch from Gulberwick, and ten glass beads from Hillswick. At Garthsbanks in Quendale there was found in 1870 in a "built ruin" six or seven silver "armlets" (really silver bullion), a horn full of 10th century Anglo-Saxon coins and "cleeber" bowls. The old Lerwick Museum supplied the National Museum with a "cleeber" vessel with a handle, and Eshaness has furnished a weight for a balance in the shape of a horse's head.

Jarlshof finds are very varied and extend over a long period, but characteristic are combs, hones, loom weights and sinkers, whorls made of the heads of ox femurs, querns, "cleeber" vessels, bone pins and bronze plates which were riveted into kettles.

Among these arts of peace and quiet years there is one which speaks of the popular reputation which the Norse receive in history. It is from Kirkhouse, Whiteness, and is a 10th century axe head.

Apart from isolated church records and undated references in the saga, Shetland history proper begins in 1299, with a document

An Outline of Shetland Archaeology

concerning Papa. At first documents were occasional, but from 1550 they are numerous, and from 1620 more than ample. But these, though of interest to every Shetlander, do not enter into an Outline of Archaeology, which is all that can be given here.

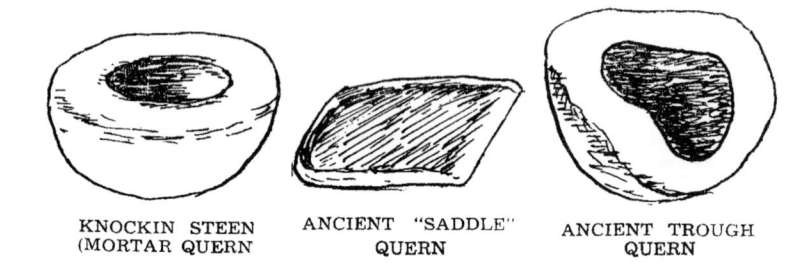

KNOCKIN STEEN (MORTAR QUERN)   ANCIENT "SADDLE" QUERN   ANCIENT TROUGH QUERN

Appendix I

SOME heel-shaped cairns (burial places). Punds-water, Mucklawater, Rönis Hill, Hamar or Houlland, Beorgs of Houster, Mangaster, "Gateside" near Hillswick, Culster, all in Northmaven. Muckle Heog in Unst. Vord Hill in Fetlar. Hill of Dale (Delting). Mill Burn (Lunning). Pettigersfield and Wart of Symbister Ness (Whalsay). Selivoe, Wart of Culswick, Wart of Silwick (Sandsting). Turdale Water and Wart of Vementry (Aithsting). Gillaburn and Grista (Tingwall). The absence in South Shetland may be due to lack of fieldwork.

Round cairns with cists (burial places). About five times as many. In all two to three hundred cairns have been recognised. Usually, like the first, on a hilltop or hill-shoulder, and often destroyed to build "warts" or watch places in Norse times, and also Ordnance Survey stations. Circular or slightly oval in shape, and particularly common in Sandsting and Aithsting and the Westside generally. All over Shetland on high ground. A proportion of those recorded are probably heel-shaped.

Small cists (burials with cremation). Although it was said earlier that Orkney small cists (stone boxes about 18 inches square containing burnt material) were rare in Shetland, there seems to be some evidence that they occur in Dunrossness. They are also recorded from Quarff. Records of such finds would be valuable.

Burnt Mounds (cooking places). Green mounds, nearly always with a cup-shaped hollow in one side, beside a burn, loch, or marsh. Nearly always in present-day "toons". They are full of burnt stones, sometimes with a "cist", which may have been an oven, were "fairy knows" in olden times, and are prominent local landmarks, though dozens have been levelled. They do not agree in place with the oldest type of houses and the cairns. One I know was close to a house with Iron Age pottery; another was near to an oval house, polished stone axes were close to a third. Might they not, to give them their rather sinister reputation later as fairy knows, have been primitive crematoriums instead of cooking places. This would give them a life from the Bronze Age to the introduction of Christianity, when burial again became the rule. Very numerous; probably two to three hundred.

Houses. A great number. About 60 to 70 of older type recognised, but only a small part of Shetland has been surveyed. Often sunk into a slope. Oval, with a hollow in the centre, and big stones showing round the edges (burnt mounds are smooth and green, without large stones). Relics of habitation are continually turning up, but are not recorded. Rude stone implements and trough querns mark each site. Pottery is usually deep; in the right hands it can help to fix the age.

The following is a list of brochs, and (in small capitals) defensive works:

Unst. Woodwick, Newgord Holm, Underhoull, BLUE MULL, Snabrough, Oganess, Burrafirth, Baliasta, Balta Isle, Colvadale, Uyeasound.

Yell. Vigon, Westsandwick, West Yell, Cuppister, Breckon, Greenbank, Burraness, Windhouse, Aywick, Gossabrough, LOCH OF KETTLESTER, Burravoe.

Fetlar. Snabrough, Brough Lodge, Houbie, Feal, STRANDIBROCH.

Whalsay. Brough, Saltness, HUXTER LOCH.

Bressay. Heogan, Leraness, Aith, Culliesbrough, Brough, Noss Sound.

Northmaven. Hamnavoe, Houlland Loch, Sae Breck, Hillswick, Orbister, Islesburgh, Fethaland, KAME OF ISBISTER, Gluss, Loch of Burraland.

Delting. BURGASTOO, Burravoe, Brough, Firths Voe.

Lunnasting. Lunna, Vidlin, BURGAWATER.

Nesting and East Tingwall. LOCH OF STAVANESS, Housabister, CORN HOLM, Brough, Benston, LOCH OF BENSTON, Railsbrough, Wadbister Ness, Hawksness, HOLM OF CALIFF.

Lerwick and South. Clickimin, Brindister, BRINDISTER LOCH, Aithsetter, Gord, Mail, Mousa, Burland, Houlland, Levenwick, Clumlie, Dalster, Voe, LAMBHOGA HEAD, Clevigarth, Virkie, SUMBURGH HEAD.

Aithsting and Sandness. East Burrafirth, Houlland, Noonsbrough, Brindister, West Burrafirth, Bousta, NESS OF GARTH, Melby Holm, Huxter.

Walls and Sandness. Watsness, Footabrough, Setter, Burland, Burgawater, Burrastow, LOCH OF KIRKIGARTH, Pinehoulland, West Houlland, Culswick, Westerskeld, Easterskeld.

Weisdale to Burra. Heglisbister, Hogaland, Stromness Voe, Burwick, Burland (Trondra), Brough, Grunasound, Houss (Burra).

West Dunrossness. Ireland, Scousburgh, Lunabist, LOCH OF BROO, Skelberry, NESS OF BURGIE, SOUGH HAVEN (Fair Isle).

Chapels. These were very numerous. Yell and Unst, for example, had three churches and parishes each; the former 24 and the latter about 20 chapels. Fetlar had one church and 10 chapels. Most of the sites and some of the dedications are known.

Appendix II

STONE Implements. Very highly polished stone implements are of three main kinds, and mostly of porphyry. First a boat-shaped celt or stone axe, once called in Shetland a thunderbolt, from the notion that it had fallen from the sky. Second a similar stone, but slightly curved and adze-shaped. Third a Shetland knife, oval or oblong with rounded corners, slate-thin and often slightly bent. The latter have more than once been found in groups of half a dozen or less, without any ruin near. A very rare stone looks like a squat, short-handled cricket bat.

Ground Implements. Rubbing stones for use with querns are ordinary big oval flattish beach stones, rubbed entirely flat on one side. Sometimes the handle or grip of a cylindrical stone is ground smaller than the rest. The commonest stone is like a blunt straight ox-horn or sperm-whale tooth.

Rough Implements. By far the greatest number. Thin oblong stones, used as hoes are commonest, then hammer stones, battered at both ends. Anvil stones are big and flat, pitted with marks where they have been hammered. Pointed stones are not uncommon, and rough balls of quartz. Rounded pot-lids and small squarish pieces of sandstone are fairly common, while biconical rubbers are like the frustra of two cones joined together at their bases. Holed flat heart-shaped or scapula shaped stones can have been hoes, but most holed stones are Iron Age loom weights or fishing gear.

Pot Boilers. Where clay pots could not stand fire, they are set in ashes, filled with liquid, and then a heated pebble was dropped in. These pebbles appear whole when found, but fall to pieces in the hand.

Flint or chert is rare in Shetland, but quartz is very common. It appears to have been broken in fire, but not much fashioned.

Steatite. Manufactured widely and exported to Orkney. If the vessel is deep or shaped like a biscuit-barrel it is early, but if bowl-shaped it may be viking. Whorls for spinning were usually steatite, and the hole is often driven obliquely to give the implement a wobble.

Querns. The ordinary hand-mill is post-Roman. The "knockin-steen", or kettle-shaped mortar, though used up to recent times, is a little older. The ancient Shetland trough quern was like a "knockin-steen" with one side broken out (scoop-shaped). There are also some flat stones, slightly hollowed, which may be called saddle-querns, though they are usually like a very shallow trough, with a rim on three sides.

Appendix III

Museums

SOME readers may have in their possession material which can build up the archaeological record. Generally such finds are of no value in themselves, and they are of little value even in a collection without a record of when, where, and in what circumstances they were found, for example, if there was any indication of a ruin, or if an isolated article had been somehow lost. A description or drawing of such a relic for the purpose of record is usually of more importance than its exhibition in a museum. Of the many finds each year very few are recorded; for example, there must be numerous polished stone axes and knives and kleeber urns which have never seen the light of print, and cannot therefore be fitted into the time scheme of archaeological.

The establishment of a museum is an urgent matter, not so much for prehistoric as for recent material, a sixareen (there was on at Brough Lodge a year or two ago), a packie of lines, huggie staff, owskerry, square-sail, rakkie, and all her equipment, a sheepskin (and dogskin), buoy, tümikins for winding ropes, and brigdies for twisting fine line. In spinning there was the Muckle wheel, which was secured to the wall, two forms of wheel, sweerie and reel, wool cards, and various forms of yard winders. In straw there were flakkies for winnowing and for horseback, various kinds of kishies (creels), (meeshie, rivvie, skep, büdie, cuddie, toyeg), simmonds (straw rope) for making these, for roofking, and for making fast cornstacks, and in olden times, in the house, a straw partition called a bulk, and in the rafters a sort of network loft called a terry. Bentgrass and rushes were also used for rope, and dockens and latterly willows for creels or kishies. Skins were used for covering the backs of horses (bendin-skin) and of humans (back-pelter) when carrying loads, in making fishing clothes and strong rope for cliff-climbing, as humlibands (grommets for oars), and as traces in ploughing, as well as various containers, from the cash to hold tobacco to the buggie, which was made of a whole sheepskin. Until lately an outfit of three sieves, one with small holes, another with larger holes, and a third without any, was used for sifting meal. All were made of sheepskin stretched on hoops. Last, but not least, there were the rivlin, or moccasin of untanned hide. Containers of wood were legion, trenchers and plates, caps and kits, saes and rubbin-tubs, bummies, kirns, fiddeks, daffeks, hurries and the rest. Wood was in use for purposes as varied as clogs, a kishie needle for straw work, a klibber or wooden saddle, a fleeter for skimming pots, a mell for crushing bere in a knockin-stane, swills (swivels) and head-parts for animals' tethers, and the bismer for weighing. How many Shetlanders now know of an avnet (for scooping up fish which escape off the hook), a huggie-staff (clip for the same purpose), a birkieclepp for tearing up tormentil or bark for preserving nets and lines, or a flachter-spade, for lifting divots for roofing thatch? Its there an old Shetland plough or scythe except in Edinburgh? Even the last thatched roof will soon be gone, and all the technique and names connected with this age-old practice will be forgotten.

On Excavation. Ruins are continually cleared away in the course of improvements. Examples which occur to me recently are a Bronze Age house at Sandwick (dam for waterworks), rude stone implements at Hamister, Whalsay (water pipes), and inhabited sites at Isbister, Whalsay, and Scousburgh (building). In such cases it is best to send all small finds, especially pottery, to the National Museum, Queen Street, Edinburgh, for identification, and to publish the finds in the local press.

Sites should be left alone unless they are being destroyed in the course of agriculture or building. There is no chance whatever of finding anything of value, and the removal even of turf may lead to the destruction of whatever stone formation is underneath and to the loss of valuable evidence.

The main purpose of archaeology is not to collect material in museums, nor renovate tumbledown sites for the benefit of tourists, but to map and describe accurately all finds from pre-history, so that a body of knowledge may be built up of how people lived in the many centuries which are gone. In the evidence still existing of these centuries Shetland is one of the fortunate lands.

APPENDIX IV

EXTRACT from a letter sent by John Stewart to his daughter Margaret and her husband Howell. 15/8/1974

    I have really made quite important discoveries in Whalsay this year. After the Symbister Ness cairn, for which I am anxiously waiting your photographs, I found another one at the north side of Houll Loch, one near the manse on the lower side of the road, one in the fence at the foot of the rigs at Whitefield, one under the ridge of rocks which runs down from the Ward of Clate about half a mile up from where we had our picnic and a "temple" sort of building in the last vicinity which can neither be classed as a dwelling nor a grave. It has no stone implements as far as I can see (necessary in a dwelling) and the chambers are round and far too big for grave goods. I visited Pettigersfield again, got your compass fixed in the notch of the winged stones and got Robert John Anderson to read the degrees of the islands round the eastern horizon which I noted. I am quite sure they had a perfect calendar here, supplemented by two or three strategically placed stones on the cliff edge as extra marks. Then one morning I had a flash of insight. The cairns are as alike as peas, all except one, and are made more alike in that each has, less than a hundred feet away a cist grave with a massive cap stone, like a stone box with stone lid. But they are all empty, no bones as in an ossuary, merely streaks of burnt stuff, such as you might find in a crematorium garden of remembrance. Now burning a body is a big messy business so where was it done. Well, there are in Whalsay mounds of burnt stone in several places, always near water. They occur in Wales (where they are called "deer roasts"), Ireland and elsewhere but nowhere so densely as in Shetland. Now if the stone age Shetlanders had a barbecue every time they wanted supper one cannot imagine what houses they lived in or what sort of social structure they must have had. So against all other Archaeologists, for I have never even heard the thing suggested, I am willing to believe that the burnt mounds were primitive burning ghats.

    When the idea occurred I was sitting out, on a beautiful morning, for Isbister. Here I met a classmate, Hugh Sutherland, Bobby's uncle. He is a

An Outline of Shetland Archaeology

very intelligent man who has a burnt mound on his croft. "What were they for?" I asked, "Cremation", he said. He told me of an old neighbour who had said so. A tradition could hardly come down 3500-4000 years, so I asked him if he had any other evidence. "Yes", he said, the stones had been subjected to intense heat, out of keeping with normal cooking process. He could often press them to dust in his hand, and he had noted wood ash as well as peat. He was able to distinguish by the fibres. I did not mention the empty cairns which had led me to the same conclusion. But it seems a much more logical and valid explanation than "deer roasts".

A REPORT concerning heel-shaped cairns, written by John Stewart. This undated handwritten report is in the Shetland Archives where it is attached to the above letter. It is on the same paper and in the same layout and style, giving it the appearance of being contemporary with the letter.

Further important discoveries have been made in the island of Whalsay by Mr John Stewart MA, FSA Scot (1942), who specialises in its archaeology, and who over a period of a year uncovered the Standing Stones of Yuxie (a so called temple), the cairn and cist on the Know of Pettigersfield, and the Bunyie Hoose. The last was excavated more massively by Mr Calder and Mr Stewart in two fortnightly periods in the years 1954-5, two men being employed on each occasion by Mr Calder and an intrusive crub for seedling cabbages being removed and the stones built clear of the site. The results are described by Mr Calder in the Proceedings of Antiquaries of 1960-61. Shortly after, Mr Stewart uncovered two pyramidical large stones set in the hillside 52 yards from the chambered cairn, and the unusually dry year, resulting in peat shrinkage has allowed these to be thoroughly examined.

The stones are set on a paving with flat vertical sides facing downhill and seawards at an angle of 120 degrees to each other. They touch closely up to the shoulders where a small sighting gap, in which a small compass was laid, enabled the whole eastern horizon with its numerous islets, supplemented by three stones set up on the cliff below in pre-historic time to be marked off as by a protractor. On each side of the stones are wings

66

formed by upright stones, the whole being uncannily like a seagull in flight. The wing tips are 21 feet apart. The hill rises steeply behind and the wings are not a façade to any construction buried in the turf behind them. The whole seems to be an excellent observation post for the rising of heavenly bodies on the eastern horizon, giving the calendar that primitive agriculturalists would need.

Using only a light spade and an iron rod for a probe, a number of heel-shaped cairns have been found at the South Water Hamars, near Whitefield, North Park near Marrister, and Maggie's Knowe on the north side of Houll Loch. These have been likened to the heel of a man's boot, with the entrance from the instep into a cruciform chamber, or to a side view of a cocked hat. Both analogies are good, except that the peaks of the hat would require to be extended much farther forward and backward. The essentials of the cairn are the heel-shape, some ten to fourteen feet, gradually topped off and rounded in to enclose a chamber (though none of the latter remained) and with the instep, containing the entrance, extended right and left to form a concave façade 30 to 40 feet long. This terminated in a peaked stone at each end.

The Whitefield cairn had an important difference. It was shallow from back to front and broader, and instead of the concave façade had two horns, not unlike a sperm whale's teeth projecting downwards to enclose a roughly-paved lemon-shaped forecourt.

With Dr and Mrs F. Howell Brown of Oban, the chamber and passage of Symbister Ness cairn was opened. The passage was ten feet long and the chamber cruciform. In every case it would seem that cremation was practised, for there was nothing to indicate inhumation yet cremation could not have been done on the spot, for there is no trace of ordinary burning.

It is almost certain that the mounds of small burnt stones called Burnt Mounds, two more of which at Marrister Burn and Symbister were discovered, are the actual burning sites. These are always beside water and from Irish and Welsh examples were described as "deer roasts". But in Shetland there were no deer to roast, nor could the inhabitants be living in a state of perpetual barbecue. Mr Hugh Sutherland, who has lived with a burnt mound on his croft all his life, brings forward two important points. The ash is fibrous, and more wood than peat. The stones were so friable that they could crush to powder in the hand, showing temperatures far beyond the range of ordinary cooking. At least fifteen of these mounds are known, but some have been removed, the latest being covered by the island airstrip.

The most extraordinary discovery is that each heel-cairn is accompanied by a so-called Bronze Age cists within a radius of 50 to 100 yards. This is a "chest" of stone which was covered with a massive capstone. All are broken down but one, but the indications are here of a façade of 12 feet, and a square cairn with concave sides. These are not round cairns in ground plan and are apart from the heel-shaped cairns. They raise problems of dating, and are so invariable that in the two cases where one is found the other is still to seek. It is to be noted that in the earlier excavated Knowe of Pettigersfield cist and heel-shaped cairn were under the same long cairn, being only 37 feet apart and linked by stone settings.

Lastly in a most inaccessible part under the Water Hamars a new "temple" has been found akin to the Standing Stones of Yuxie, but whereas the latter showed abundant traces of being at one time lived in, in the shape of grain rubbers and many rough stone implements, the newly-discovered building consists almost entirely of orthostatic foundations (stones set upright like the teeth in a jaw) covering an area of about 30 feet diameter whose outer bounds are not yet found. Indications are of a Trefoil head of three circles which seems to stand at an angle of 40 degrees to a rough passage leading 16 feet to a façade 12 feet wide. The circles are 7 to 9 feet in diameter. There are no indications of habitation in the form of rude stones implements, and no obvious places in the vicinity to which stones could have been removed while inhumation and cremation seem both ruled out by the plan. One of the circles was excavated many years ago, but nothing was found.

Appendix V

Excavation of a Cairn at Houll Loch, Whalsay (a handwritten report by John Stewart dated August 1935. Unfortunately the plan which he refers to in the text does not seem to have survived).

Report on Cairn – W side Houll Loch, Whalsay, Shetland.

Distance from loch 40yds. 10' above loch level. 122' above sea level.

1. History

   Entirely under peat in pre-war times. Exposed by cutting. Appeared as mound of stones 4' to 6' high. The stones were nearly all of a size possible of handling by one man. The mound was utilised by a crofter about a dozen years ago to construct a "crub" for seedling cabbages. Its form was entirely destroyed. A few loose stones were left above the turf. Practically all the mound was removed, except a few bigger stones. Since its destruction more stones have appeared on the surface with the 'packing' of loose earth, but these have been disturbed and shifted as they appeared. The condition of the structure when explored was as follows. About a dozen or so of large stones, set on end, appeared above the surface, and 50 or 60 others were scattered about without form or position.

2. Purpose of Exploration

   To discover any form in the structure, whose ultimate destruction was merely a matter of a few years. Secondarily, to preserve the form discovered pending a more thorough exploration.

3. Procedure

   Loose surface stones removed and built clear of site. Turf removed to expose stones of structure. Many of these had been removed to the underlying clay: many were so disturbed that the original shape was difficult to trace. All large stones were left in place. Chamber walling was left undisturbed, and later protected as far as possible by laying the loose surface stones first removed on top of it.

AN OUTLINE OF SHETLAND ARCHAEOLOGY

4. **Structure of Cairn**

The cairn was originally of no great height, and if it had contained lintelled passages or covered chambers all trace of these had disappeared, with the possible exception of Chamber A which had a partition-like slab at the W end, and more pronounced walling than the other chambers. A also differed from the others in being almost entirely clear of stones in the inside. An ill-defined axis ran east and west through A & B; there was a second line of extreme length from NW to SE. As far as explored the structure contained 4 chambers unsymmetrically arranged, and there is a possibility of a fifth chamber in a part unexplored, between D and B, but the fact that there is no great depth of earth here renders this doubtful.

Want of symmetry was further shown by (1) large stones set on end being confined to the N side, (2) entrances seemingly on the N side, (3) a single "horn" of clumsy, shapeless stones on the NW, (4) an area of underground drains in the SE. The fourth is explained by the character of the slope; the SW and NW sectors being the higher parts of the structure.

5. **Character of Walling, etc.**

The chambers were defined by stones with a flat face of about a foot square; there being placed side by side with the flat face inwards, so as to form a roughly hexagonal, oval or circular enclosure from 4 to 6 feet in diameter. A cell had traces of horizontal walling above these, and also a septal stone; the others did not. Everywhere the structure was filled with stones (none being under about 6" diameter), flattish, and laid horizontally and loosely layer upon layer, so that the stones of the upper layer covered the cavities between those below. But there were no regular layers, and the depth would not have been anywhere more than three stones' breadth. (These layers had been much disturbed, probably recently.)

The more shapeless and massive stones appeared to be round about the margins.

"Lintels"

A peculiarity at the ends and at the supposed entrances was that above these layers of stones, obviously lying in situ, were lintel stones as if for the roof of a passage. These were obviously too high for a threshold. It seems to me that this is a degenerate form of passage, with 'lintels' laid down though there was no opening underneath for them to bridge. The purpose was not drainage, as the layers underneath were perfectly dry.

Drains

In the SE sector, taking water from the south and also from the west were exceptionally well-built drains, square in section, and sunk into the clay "channel" to their full depth. The two investigated appeared to be in six foot lengths, roughly at right angles. There was sludge in the bottom, and the drains were full of water, rendering further investigation impossible. The sides were stones set on edge, and remaining absolutely perpendicular, the lintels were particularly huge and flat, and from the closeness with which they met they were evidently dressed at the edges. All gaps were 'blinded' by smaller flat stones, and the drains were perfectly clear of so much as even a pebble.

Cremations

Cremations where they occurred were above flat stones lying on the clay. There was about half an inch of reddish ash generally with abundant bone ash above. The most surprising thing of all was the limited space (a foot or so in diameter) occupied by each cremation. The ash when first revealed had a particularly bright red appearance, so much so that the first find was regarded as pigment or disintegrated red pottery. It would be interesting to know if the ash is wood or peat. A quantity has been kept for analysis.

Chambers in Detail

A – The north side here did not show the same careful walling as the rest, where the stones were carefully set on edge and covered by horizontal building (form of upper wall destroyed). The presumed entrance was at the east end, where 2 massive stones, the one on the S side perpendicular, that on the north slanting at 45o. Below lay a huge lintel superposed on a smaller flat stone, under which was a cremation. The floor of A slanted steeply towards (1) where many urn fragments were found.

The passage from A to B was ill-defined, the shading showing where more lumpy stones seemed to mark the sides. It was entirely filled with layers of stones. I regarded it as possible to find a small chamber here, but there was no sign of any such thing. Throughout the passage were abundant traces of burnt stones, but no definite cremation.

B - The S side of Chamber B was well defined by stones set on edge as in A. The N side had to the eastward 3 boulders on edge flanking an entrance, and on the west side of this entrance, 2 massive stones lying horizontally one on top of the other. The entrance itself had the usual "lintels" lying on layers of flat stones. Another side entrance with "lintels" seemed to lead into the passage from A to B. At (3) was found a cremation, with fragments and a stone club and axe; at (4) a piece of urn of a cremation, at (5) a cremation with abundant bone ash.

Ends

The east and W ends of the cairn had greater quantities of stone, and again the peculiar feature of large flat "lintels" was apparent. The NW end had a "horn" of clumsy boulders laid without the usual care, but on test, proving to be laid to the underlying clay. The whole of the east end was not explored owing to the presence of water.

C - Chamber C was defined in the usual way, but in this case the stone faces were at an angle, instead of almost perpendicular. So far as investigated it had no relics. A dotted line is used on the plan because, owing to my mislaying certain measurements, the actual position of the chamber cannot be given.

D - The position of this is also approximate for the above reason. Here we found 2 peculiar stone objects of triangular shape, given as No. 3 in the appended list. The sides were defined as usual and the chamber full of the usual flat stones.

Stone

1 - Rude stone club (local stone) 9?" long. Found with urn cremation at (3).

2 - Rude stone axe (point broken) 10" long. Found at (3)

3 – 2 flattish triangular stones 8"x8"x6?" x 7"x7"x7". Found together in D at (7)
4 – Smooth oval sandstone object 3?"x1?"x1/3". Found at (6)
5 – Assumed rough borer 5?" long. Cell B.
6 – Triangular borer 5" long. Cell B.
7 – Triangular point 2" long. Cell B.
8 – Flat stone disc 7"x4?" Cell B. Also disc 6"x5" Cell B. Others found were at first thrown away, to the number of 2 or 3.
9 – Oval smooth stone – broken 4"x2?"x1?". Cell B.
10 – 3 portions of a similar stone.
11 – Round quartz-like strike a-light chipped at ends. Cell B at (4).
12 – 3 leaf shaped quartz chips.]
13 – Small rounded quartz pebble   ] A, B & passage.
14 – Half of smooth stone – broken, surface disintegrated. Cell B.

Ash
15 – Stone with part of cremation layer above. Cell B (4).
16 – Ball Of ash. Cell A (2).
17 – Ball of bone ash. Cell B (5).

Bone
18 – 1 chip 1?" long. Found where rubbish had been thrown. Perhaps not from cairn.

Pottery
19 – 19 fragments of a thick vessel or vessels. Cell A (1).
20 – 8 fragments of plain-lipped thin vessel. Cell A.
21 – 3 pieces. (1) Lip. (2) Bottom edge. (3) Thick portion. Cell A.
22 – 1 piece showing trace of bead or curved lip. Cell B (4).
23 – 12 minute parts (including 1 bottom portion). Cell B (3).

The floors of the chambers were filled in with rubbish & stones & turf laid above so as to retain the outline. Everything, except the layers of stones, was replaced in the original position as nearly as possible. The finds would no doubt have been more extensive if the cairn had been entirely dug out, but this was not the purpose. It was impossible, of course, to lay each stone in the layers exactly in place, but they were put, as far as possible, where found.

Remarks on Finds

No. 3 - The two stones mentioned here were found side by side, and obviously cut to the same shape. Their purpose, whether implement, weapon, or dish is a mystery.

No. 4 - The smooth oval sandstone is foreign to the district it must be some symbolical offering.

No. 8 - These were regarded as natural at first and some were thrown away.

Nos 9 & 10 - No. 10 was found first. It was an oval smooth stone, size and shape as No. 9, and displayed the same cracks on its surface. As there are no smooth pebbles at the Loch nor nearer than the shore over a mile away, I was going to keep the stone. But it broke in pieces in my hand, so I threw it down among earth and rubbish, where it was soon covered up. A little later I came across No. 9, and laid it aside, noting it was a similar stone, but not noticing the cracks, which were hidden by peat. I only found this out when I washed the stone the same evening. I spent some time the following day searching for the parts of No. 10 but only found 3 fragments. Evidently the stones were some symbolic offering, deliberately broken. No. 14 was part of a larger smooth stone, broken by fire? The smooth surface of which crumbled away when it was removed from its bed of peat.

Nos 12 & 13 - There were many small pieces of quartz, but as the stones of the cairn have quartz encrustations the number did not seem excessive. No 12 is retained because of it shapes, No. 13 was the only smooth quartz pebble.

Nos 15, 16 & 17 - Retained for analysis. The ash was a bright red in colour. It would be interesting to know whether wood or peat ash.

Nos 19 to 23 – In spite of all efforts to keep parts separate some confusion may have taken place. Greyish pottery was shiny black when recovered from peat. Piece of lip (No 21) was clean cut with sharp edges.